D1304244

Contents At a Glance

To all Mac programmers everywhere

BYTE's Mac Programmer's Cookbook

Rob Terrell

Osborne **McGraw-Hill**

Berkeley · New York · St. Louis · San Francisco · Auckland
Bogotá · Hamburg · London · Madrid · Mexico City · Milan
Montreal · New Delhi · Panama City · Paris · São Paulo
Singapore · Sydney · Tokyo · Toronto

Osborne **McGraw-Hill**
2600 Tenth Street
Berkeley, California 94710
U.S.A.

For information on software, translations, or book distributors outside of the U.S.A., please write to Osborne **McGraw-Hill** at the above address.

BYTE's Mac Programmer's Cookbook

  234567890 DOC 9987654

ISBN 0-07-882062-6

Publisher	**Illustrator**
Lawrence Levitsky	Marla Shelasky
Acquisitions Editor	**Series Design**
Scott Rogers	Ruffin Prevost
Project Editor	**Cover Designer**
Cindy Brown	Jamie Davison Design, Inc.
Computer Designer	
Peter F. Hancik	

Contents

3: Trouble in Hacksville: When Good Macs Go Bad 27

4: Altering Reality: Utilities for a Better Life 43

Part II: The Hard Stuff

5: External Commands: Help for the Working Stiff 79

6: Ciphers and Secret Messages: Programming Languages 111

Acknowledgments

Thanks to Bob and Nancy Terrell, from whose computer store I stole most of my programming books from while just a wee tot, and whose customers taught me how to program while the other kids were outside getting fresh air and sunshine.

Heartfelt thanks to friends who made the grueling work of writing this book almost fun. To Jason Torchinsky, Kat Cook, and Charlie McGrath for the read-throughs, late-night Waffle House sessions, and the seemingly endless supply of caffeine and the occasional beer that helped me get through.

at Osborne: Scott Rogers, who hated playing the heavy as much as I hated playing the heavied. You're a much nicer guy than your receptionist had led me to believe. Larry Levitsky, who believed in this project from the outset and is a great guy to boot. Cindy Brown, who made sure my writing didn't betray my apparently near-total ignorance of proper English diction.

Thanks to folks who don't even know me: To David Smith, for putting out such a cool magazine—*MacTutor*—for so long. To Scott Boyd, whose articles in the early *MacTutor* taught me more about good programming than any of the classes I ever took. To Andy Hertzfeld, who treated me like a human being when at the age of 14 I asked him stupid questions on the MacWorld show floor. And all the other Mac gurus who never failed to supply wisdom in a moment of need.

A special thanks goes out to the members of the Van Gogh-Goghs, the sketch comedy troupe I'm a member of. While we never canceled a show due to this book, I was certainly less funny and more cranky.

Jason
Galen
Charles
T.Mike

Thanks for putting up with me.

and

a big block of thanks: Charles Overbeck, Robin Monteith, Sam Radel, Leonard Buck, Glenn Clingroth, Bob Beckett, Larry Harris, Uncle Dave Moffet, Tom Wimbish, Chris Ogden, Mary Whitesides, Hal Hartley, Ross McIlwee, Soylen T. Green, Admiral Tommy Veers (Ret.), Carl Stewart, David Skeels, Paul Philion, Mike Morrison, Tim Greening, Gary and Bonnie Moore. All you wonderful denizens of comp.sys.mac.programmer: this book's for you.

And finally, to Ruffin Prevost, who I honestly don't know how to thank, except with a bottle of Wild Turkey and a really big check. I wouldn't be writing today if it weren't for Ruffin. Truly a best friend while he was in Chapel Hill and sorely missed now that he's moved on to the big time.

Cool things that made this book happen:

Tom Waits - The Black Rider
They Might Be Giants - Apollo 18
Maria McKee -You Gotta Sin To Be Saved
Geezer Lake - Feet In Mud Again
Mile Davis & Quincy Jones - Live at Montreux
Fishbone - Give a Monkey a Brain
Mazzy Star - So That Tonight I Might See
The Internet
June - those killer live shows
Mountain Dew, Sam Adams Cream Ale

Cool things that almost destroyed this book:

The Internet
June - those time-consuming live shows
Sam Adams Cream Ale

Myst
Iron Helix
The X-Files
UNC Men's Basketball
The Simpsons
Wired Magazine, which always managed to arrive just
before a deadline

011010 11000110 0011010 11001001 100010001

011010 11000110 0011010 11001001 100010001

0011010 11001001 100010001

The Easy Stuff

Tricks of the Trade: Secrets of the Shadow Warriors

When Steve Jobs's Macintosh hit the computer scene in 1984, it set the standard for human-machine interaction for at least a decade. But it had one minor problem: it was a closed box with limited software. And there was no way to write new software on it. But that didn't deter the hackers.

From the very first days, the true supporters of the Macintosh were hackers. Most early adopters emigrated from the Apple II world—people who'd become part of the cult of the 6502, graphic artists, designers, and others who couldn't relate to the Intel-dominated world of the time and fell for the first Macintosh, despite the conventional wisdom of the day. These mavericks bucked the system, using their Macintoshes to do the impossible.

Quote

This book is for the people of the United States of America....
Radical groups don't need this book. They already know
everything that's in here. If the real people of America, the
silent majority, are going to survive, they must educate
themselves. That is the purpose of this book.
—William Powell, in the foreword to The Anarchist Cookbook

3

For some reason these mavericks fell in love with the jumble of circuits and wires that Steve Jobs's Macintosh team built. Jobs pushed his people hard, and they produced a machine to be proud of. But after the strain of the production effort, the team could not continue the pace and intensity—team members were too drained and burned out to focus on software for their new creation.

So in the early years, programming and developer support from Apple was weak at best. Users could rely on the existing dealer network to answer questions and solve problems. But hackers? Ah, that's another story.

The Mac Hacker Culture

Apple sold a Macintosh development system that was actually Apple's $10,000 Lisa computer. This was not the way to make friends in the developer community. Few of the early adopters, folks who jumped ship from their $2000 Apple IIs, could afford such a luxury. So they used their considerable skills to make up for what they lacked in bucks (a key principle of the hacker ethic). Through a combination of brute force, finesse, and sheer programming talent, the early Mac hackers slowly began to pry their way into the closed Macintosh.

that "against all odds" mentality is the spirit that inspired this book. "The power to be your best," as the old Apple ads went. This cookbook is designed to provide you with the instructions and ingredients you need to make your Macintosh the best tool it can be. Whether you plan to explore your Mac's potential or write better programs faster, this book is your source for tasty code recipes.

In the 1960s, *The Anarchist Cookbook* provided a sourcebook tuned to the tenor of the times. In its pages, you could find recipes for marijuana brownies, pipe bombs, and phone taps. These were the tools of the revolutionary, fighting the invisible oppression, fighting to take control.

Today, a different revolution is taking place, a grassroots digital uprising. Consider this cookbook your call to arms in the new revolution. Take control of your computer. No longer be oppressed by its strange ways; no longer be powerless to control it. A computer is a tool—an incredibly varied and flexible multipurpose tool—but still just a tool. You can easily learn all it takes to master it.

Never Underestimate the Power of Hacks

The nice thing about a big computer industry is that no matter what problem you encounter, chances are someone has already solved it. There are very few original problems. However, many of the problems you'll encounter as a programmer require especially clever solutions. You can come up with one of these clever solutions or sit back and discover how some hacker has already solved the problem for you.

Got to get up off of that thing. Yeah. Get on it.

—James Brown

Consider the PowerBook cursor dilemma. When PowerBooks first came out, everyone had the same complaint: the thin, faint "I-beam" cursor was difficult to see against the liquid crystal screen. So how did smart people solve the problem? They waited a week or two until even smarter people wrote a whole host of hacks to make the cursor more visible and posted their extensions and control panels on online services.

The key is to know where smart people hang out, and hang out with them.

As I finish this first chapter, the Macintosh is celebrating its tenth birthday. That's a decade of smart people playing with their Macintoshes, running into problems, and finding clever ways around them. You don't have ten years to catch up!

This book shows you how to be more productive through the use of really clever things that smart people have been doing for ten years. Whether you're a spreadsheet jockey or a total code warrior, some hacker probably solved your specific problems years ago. This book gives you those solutions; it's up to you to use them.

What the Heck Is a Hack?

In this book I'll be referring to *hacks* quite a bit. What is a hack? I'm glad you asked:

Hack (hak) vt. **1.** *to chop or cut crudely* **2.** *a harsh, dry cough* **3.** *[slang] to carry out or manage something successfully*

- a clever, elegant, inspired, or inventive solution to a problem

- a piece of programming code that achieves the impossible, or at least the improbable

- just plain old brute force—the ultimate hack

The term *hack* isn't always confined to computerdom; you'll find computer people referring to other things (such as cold fusion and all Sony products) as hacks, too. And it's usually a compliment.

Breaking the code

When I refer to code, I'm talking about computer programming. For some reason, computer programs are referred to as code, perhaps due to their near-illegibility to the lay person.

From time to time, I'll show actual examples of programming code. Code will appear in a special typeface to set it off from the body of the chapter.

```
The code will look like this.
It will appear in this monospaced typeface.
```

The Good, the Bad, and the Ugly

Sometimes, though, calling something a hack isn't always a compliment. You've got to learn the gestalt. There are good hacks and ugly hacks.

It is impossible to predict the time and progress of revolution. It is governed by its own more or less mysterious laws.

—Lenin

I have a cordless Sony Walkman; it sends the music to the headphone via radio waves, so there's no cord to get tangled. That's a neat hack. I also have a portable Sony CD player that plugs into my car's tape deck through a weird and cumbersome cassette-tape-shaped plug. That's an ugly hack.

This terminology applies in the computer world as well. Virex, which traps disk-insertion events and uses the opportunity to scan for viruses, is a neat hack. ClickLock, which simulates a locking button for your mouse or trackball, does so by mucking about with the system's low-memory globals. It's an ugly hack. But it works—for now at least.

Ugly hacks depend on undocumented features that the programmer exploits. Low-memory globals, for instance, are not very well documented, and Apple sternly warns programmers to avoid playing with them, since one day they all may change. But some of the best hacks—ugly hacks, all—depend upon low-memory globals to work their magic.

no one knows for sure what will happen to ugly hacks when the system changes. How likely is that? Well, ever hear of the PowerPC? As Apple moves its Macintosh product line to Motorola's new RISC chip, all bets are off, low-memory-globalwise. I guarantee that many ugly hacks will disappear when that day comes.

Give me back my name

Way back—and I mean way back, like in 1982—the term "hacker" was a good word. It was a blessing you bestowed upon your friends sparingly, when you really liked them, and only if they were really good programmers. People were proud to be hackers. I remember thinking of myself as a hacker. (At the age of 11, I also thought a plastic pocket protector was a good idea. I didn't realize how close I came to being a geek, but that's another story.)

Thanks to our sensationalist and largely ignorant mass media, the term "hacker" has been taken away from us. It's still used inside the circle in the manner in which it was intended. Someone could say, "That Bill Atkinson, now there's a true hacker," with a wistful gleam in one's eye. Inside the circle we understand that Bill's a cool guy, a total genius, a programmer extraordinaire. The man speaks in 68000 assembly, his dreams have a vertical blanking interrupt. But to call him a hacker today (at least in "mixed" company) would imply that he's a criminal.

You don't usually call people hackers anymore, unless they've been one for a long time, or tend to practice sleep-deprivation coding, eat meals comprised entirely of junk food, and wear Microsoft T-shirts. And mostly it's a comment about lifestyle, not programming prowess.

Well, scrog that. Let's take back the term. It belongs to us—the real hackers, from an age long since gone—the crazy people who gave the computer industry to Wall Street. They can keep the corporate culture—just give us back our name.

Whither Hack?

So why do you want hacks in your life?

- **They can make your life easier.** Who wants to keep your finger on the mouse button all day? Get ClickLock and forget about it. Why move the mouse six inches when three will do? Get Mouse2 and delay carpal tunnel syndrome for another day.

- **They can make your life richer.** Why shell out big bucks for development environments when you can get shareware versions that work just as well and cost nothing?

- **They can make your life longer.** Who wants to write the code necessary to create full-color, full-motion, multilayer game sprites? Maybe some freak computer maniac who hasn't left his basement in six years, but personally, I've got better things to do with my time—like focusing on the game itself, not the graphics programming.

To stand against a C of troubles

Right now, despite the attempts of rational, sane people, the C programming language is the most popular language in use for the Macintosh. For those of you unfamiliar with it, C is a vile, strange, unfriendly beast, a witch's brew of unintuitive commands and silly rules.

Computers have been growing more powerful at a geometric rate. The computer I'm typing on is probably the functional equivalent of all the computers of the 1974 Hungarian government.

Ancient computers were programmed in antiquated ways, using punch cards and paper tape, in obscure and difficult languages. We've tossed the silly paper cards, but we're still using ancient and abstruse languages.

My dad worked for AT&T about the time they came up with C and UNIX. My dad (still) programs in C. I don't want my dad's old suits with the flared pants nor do I want his programming language. (However, I do covet his '65 Mustang convertible and original Elvis albums.)

The conventional wisdom seems to be, "harder is better." This is ridiculous. And it will end. Mark my words—you heard it here first.

A whole host of new languages, from Kaleida Lab's ScriptX to the new object-oriented Pink operating system from Taligent, will fly into a no-holds barred, fists-of-fury free-for-all with C. And when C is banished from respectable programming circles, I'll be the head of the cheerleading squad.

I've Never Paid for it in My Life

One important thing to remember is that nothing is free. Well, okay, water is free to me and everyone in my apartment complex, but besides that, nothing is free.

Many hack-creators—dare I say hackers?—will release their programs to the world for free. Sometimes, if you're a programmer, they may ask for a mention in your program's About Box or documentation. In that case, you're in luck.

Some hacks are categorized as "postcardware", "beerware," or "fill-in-the-blank-ware." The basic premise is "Hey, I've just written this cool hack that you're using, so you send me a postcard or a six-pack of beer or whatever." I can't imagine that this works well, but it's probably a brilliant way to get beer if you're an underage programmer. (Oddly enough, I've never heard of "Penthouseware.")

But as often as not, a hack will be shareware. Shareware is a unique concept by which you can acquire the software via any means—from an online service, from a friend's hard drive or floppy, from an act of God—and use it free for a period of time. When the time's up, if you decide to keep it, you've gotta pay up.

It's an amazing testament to the human race that it works at all. Sadly, it rarely does work. I've spoken with dozens of shareware authors who are broke, while their program has been downloaded hundreds or even thousands of times from CompuServe or America Online.

but a rare few authors actually make some money at it. Sometimes it's their livelihood. They check the mailbox every day, their eyes alive with the hopes of finally receiving a few piddling checks.

Here's the litmus test. Call your mom and ask her what you should do. Think about how the conversation would go: "Hi, Mom, guess what I did today? I got this really neat program that I didn't pay a dime for! I'm ripping off that poor hardworking sucker!" If you can live with your conscience, well, then, I guess you're like all those other people who are downloading shareware and not paying for it. But that doesn't make it right. (And I think your mom would agree.)

A shiny red bicycle

Remember the Red Bicycle Movement? No, of course you don't, because no one does. The Red Bicycle Movement was a turn-of-the-century effort toward benevolent Marxism. The Movement bought hundreds of bicycles, painted them bright red, and distributed them throughout the city. The idea was that if you needed to get somewhere, you could grab a red bicycle and just go. When you reached your destination, you left it so someone else could use it.

As you'd expect, in about three weeks, every red bicycle was stolen and hocked to some used-bicycle-consortium in the islands, leaving the townspeople a little bewildered and a little less mobile, and leaving our idealistic heroes in the movement dispirited and broken people, who probably began to cheat on their taxes.

If you can't see the moral of this story, call your mom right now and ask her to explain it to you. You might also ask her to explain the moral fine points of a seven-state killing spree while you're at it...you see, there aren't any fine points to a killing spree, it's pretty cut and dried, and so is shareware.

The Cookbook Manifesto

This book is for people who use and work with Macintoshes on a practical level. It is not written for an elite inner circle of high Mac druids, lifetime subscribers of *Mac Tech Magazine,* or Leonard Rosenthal. Those radical groups don't need this book. They already know everything that's in here, or at least think they do. If the real Mac users of America, the silent majority who blush when they buy books with titles like *More Crazy Mac Tricks for Brain-Dead Idiots* want

In this world a man must either be anvil or hammer.

—Longfellow

to survive, then they must educate themselves. That is the purpose of this book.

Hacks are for everyone. They just take a bit of snooping around to find them, and a bit of knowledge to use them effectively. Even if you've just joined the Macintosh revolution, you'll need a few tools. And even if you've been programming for years—like I have—you can always use a smart friend to do the tough stuff for you.

This book is divided into two sections: the easy stuff and the hard stuff. The easy stuff is filled with hacks that make your life easier—things that anyone can use, today, to make their computing experience better, richer, and more productive.

the hard stuff is for more advanced folks, those who actually program the Mac. Finding the right hacks can be the key between a five-hour project and a week-long nightmare. If you had to write all the XCMDs that Frederick Rinaldi gives away for free, you'd be insane, muttering to yourself incoherently like that vagrant behind the Exxon station. Frederick Rinaldi is a smart guy. Don't redo all the work he's done. Borrow from him. Just like they taught you in school, in real life you can do very well if you learn to cheat properly.

Coming Up Next

Now that you know what a hack is, the next question is: where are they? In Chapter 2, "Getting the Goods," we'll talk about the places to find great hacks: from bulletin boards to user groups to commercial services. What do you look for? Where's the best place to find the hack *you* need?

Welcome to the revolution. Next we'll be issuing supplies. Pay attention: the successful computer warrior chooses weapons carefully. Don't lag behind, or you'll fall prey to the adversaries on all sides. We're going to suit up in bug-proof Kevlar, load one in the chamber, switch off the safeties, and start nailing some first-class hacks.

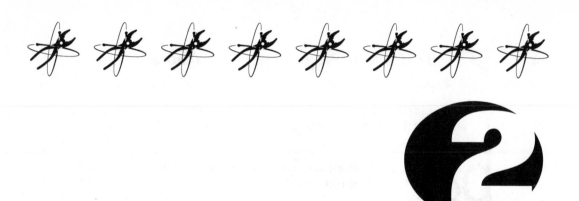

Getting the Goods

Welcome to the code wars. We're heading into dangerous territory, the hangouts and hiding places of hackers, crackers, and nuts. We're going deep into uncharted regions, so stay close; I'll be your guide. Don't lose your step! Don't fall behind! In cyberspace, no one can hear you scream.

in this chapter we're going to show you the way to the best hacks, the crème de la crème, the dopest, flyest, most helpful shareware in the realm. For the last ten years, really great hackers have been learning the secrets of the Mac ROMS, spelunking 68000 code in the dead of night, losing their eyesight from staring at nine-inch screens. They've learned these suckers inside and out, and their efforts have provided you with these resources. Use them. Respect them.

Once Upon a Time in the Net

Ask not what, but what for.
—Ed Poindexter

My first modem was a Hayes 300-baud modem that plugged into an S-100 bus computer called the Exidy Sorcerer. (Remember Exidy? It once made console-style video games. Now, it's just another fallen warrior in the personal computer hardware wars.) Back then, CompuServe was fighting for the computer-communications market with a company called the Source. (CompuServe swallowed the Source whole not so

long ago—another victim of the computer content-provider wars.) I used the Source because I had a free demo account.

back then, chatting with other users was the focus of online services. The Source let you chat with one person at a time; CompuServe had a "CB Simulator" that let many people converse at once, using "handles" to identify themselves. (This was so long ago, CB radio was still considered hip and cutting edge.)

At some point the focus shifted. Online chatting, while still an important part of the whole experience, fell from grace among hardcore hackers. The online file library became the Holy Grail of service providers: whoever could have the biggest, baddest, most eclectic collection of files for downloading would rule the online universe.

See you in cyberspace

In 1986, William Gibson wrote a book called Neuromancer, in which he coined the word cyberspace. Cyberspace perfectly describes the universe of computer connections created by the explosion of technology in the fields of telephony, modems, and computers. (Not a bad book, either. Rob says read it. Real hackers already own the Voyager interactive hypertext version.)

When this book mentions cyberspace, I'm talking about the Internet, or even more generally, the entire superset of electronic computer communications of which the Internet is merely a part. When I'm talking about "the net," I mean the collection of online services, bulletin boards, and cyberspaces where programmers and hackers hang out. But sometimes, "the net" is just a convenient abbreviation for the Internet. You may have to figure it out from context.

Online Services and the Single Hacker

These days, it's hard *not* to be a member of an online service. What with the software and online time given away free with modems, and the massive PR blitzes culminating in a barrage of annoying ads for an array of information superhighway-based services, you've got to tread carefully to avoid being snared in the net. (No pun intended.)

but you ought to join an online service because it really is the best way to learn more about your computer. Online services are to today's communication network what swamps were to the American Revolution—a retreat full of independents and radicals, the last refuge of scoundrels, the birthplace of guerrilla fighting tactics. Head for the online services to get the straight dope on all that matters (and much that doesn't).

Plus, online is where the files are. All sorts of shareware, freeware, beerware, postcardware, and otherware lie archived in these huge electron vaults. It's easy for any anarchist programmer to waltz in and pick and choose from the thousands and thousands of programs.

There are six major online services:

- **CompuServe** The oldest and the biggest, the monster shark that swallowed all of its competition, CompuServe has a well-deserved reputation for being complicated, although it offers software with a graphical user interface (the CompuServe Information Manager, as well as the CompuServe Navigator) that does a good job of hiding much of the complexity.

2

- **America Online** The dolphin—that is, the mortal enemy of the shark—AOL is making a decent run at besting CompuServe. Its file libraries and user base are not as large or diverse as CompuServe's, but they're certainly big enough to accommodate the needs of most users. I use AOL daily for personal and business tasks.

- **Prodigy** The great experiment of IBM and Sears, this service has been hemorrhaging money for years and has become a bit of an online joke. Prodigy makes you pay for the service, and then fills your screen with ads. Plus, the folks at Prodigy reserve the right to censor people's messages. There's really no compelling reason to use Prodigy over the other online services.

- **GEnie** Run by General Electric, GEnie has been an also-ran for so long it hurts my brain just to think about it. This service has started offering a nice graphical user interface along the lines of America Online or the CompuServe Information Manager, which should improve its chances in the online service wars. There is good Mac support from a cluster of helpful Mac fanatics.

- **AppleLink** Apple's private information toll road has been around for years. Originally it was created for Apple dealers, distributors, and salespeople, and quickly became the main place for Mac developers to hang out and ask questions. Although its popularity has waned in recent years (mostly due to its outrageous $37.50 per hour access charges), it's still a great place to look for wisdom. If you are in the Apple certified Developer program (which means you pony up $1200 a year to Apple), you can submit programming questions to Apple Developer Technical Support via AppleLink and quickly get an answer you can trust. But it's too pricey for most of us.

- **Delphi** My personal favorite online service is making a comeback. Recently Rupert Murdoch bought Delphi, and the top-notch Delphi programming team has a chance to strut its stuff by integrating Murdoch's other holdings (20th Century Fox Television programs and countless magazines) online. Delphi was one of the first commercial online services to offer extensive access to the Internet. Keep an eye out for these guys: they're going places fast.

Prodigy, the wonder flub

I refuse to use Prodigy. When I tried the service (soon after it started), it didn't support the Mac interface. Being a Mac user, I found myself unable to return to a world where cut, copy, and paste were things only kindergartners were allowed to do. I'm sure Prodigy has added a nice, Apple-compliant user interface by now, but I was offended by those early lame attempts at attracting customers.

Plus, I can't stand the continuous stream of on-screen advertisements. When I pay for a TV channel—like HBO— I don't have to see ads. (Except, I suppose, for HBO's own plugs.) When I don't pay for a channel, like WTBS, I know I'll have to sit through hundreds of brain-numbing and insulting ads for expectorants.

When you're in Prodigy, some ad lies in some corner of your screen at every moment. (Even TV hasn't gotten that bad. Yet.) Who was the genius at Prodigy who thought up the idea of charging me to watch ads? This guy probably thinks the moon landing was faked and that pro wrestling is real. Wake up! Americans may have extremely short attention spans but we're not stupid! Prodigy's minuscule member numbers and waning market share prove that there is hope left for America.

There are a few others worth mentioning. Apple licensed technology from America Online and launched eWorld in an attempt to create an online dynasty. Apple already has their online service (see above), but it's very expensive and not aimed at regular users. eWorld will someday encompass the existing AppleLink system, and if Apple has its wishes, take over the markets of some other services as well. If you're a Mac hacker, it may be worth your while to check it out.

the WELL, or Whole Earth 'Lectronic Link (try to refrain from gagging at the cutesy name), has been very popular with true hackers, underground subversives, and Grateful Dead fans. It's a place to see and be seen. It offers Internet connectivity to and from the net, so you can get the usual Internet services from the WELL, or get to the WELL from your usual Internet connection. There's not a strong focus on a software library, since WELL subscribers represent a diverse array of computing hardware. It's worth a look, if nothing else.

Cyberspace on Less Than $25 a Month

There's only one electronic frontier that's still wild, untamed, unregulated, and mostly unexploited by corporate America: the Internet. If you haven't heard about the Internet, welcome back to the planet, and how is the Andromeda galaxy anyway? The Internet has become the focus of the national debate on America's information infrastructure, thanks to Slick Willie and Stiff Al.

At its most basic, the Internet is a large number of government, military, and mostly university computers interconnected through various networking schemes, all using a common way of sending data (the TCP/IP protocol). From this base, many services have grown: e-mail, so you can send a message to your buddy in Alaska instantly; FTP, so you can browse through software collections at hundreds of sites; WAIS (wide area information search), so you can search for an information needle in a digital haystack; plus the incredibly popular newsgroups, which have become universally accepted to the point of being almost unwieldy, so that you can discuss topics with your electronic neighbors.

while it's great for politicians to notice something and frame a national policy around it, what truly sucks is that someone may decide that they actually own it, and try to control it. It's already happening—more and more big corporations are joining the net. And there's a bill winding its way through Congress that will sell off parts of the Internet, just like so many parcels of land from the Northwest Territories.

Who do you want running the net?

Consider how these two extremely different entities view the information infrastructure:

To a hacker: The Information Infrastructure = the cross connection of computers and services to make the world a better place.

To big conglomerates: The Information Infrastructure = the cross connection of computers and services to suck the money out of American households 24 hours a day.

Who do you want in charge of the Internet? (Hint: there is a right answer.)

Freedom of the press [and the net] belongs to those who own it.
—Ruffin Prevost

The Internet is dying, folks. Some old-timers might even say it's already dead. Some view it as less of a death than a transformation, but to those of us who've been there a while, any change is frightening and threatening.

As of 11:58 A.M. on January 5, 1994, the Internet is still the best place to find clever hacks, obscure and nifty programming languages, and smart friends. So until the boys in Washington sell off the whole thing to Time-Warner so they can make it into an interactive version of "Jeopardy!," get plugged in.

How to Make SmartFriends and Influence People

If you're not already online—plugged in, modeming, wired, use whatever term you like—your competition has an advantage that you can only imagine. The online world has been a source of software, support, and gossip for as long as there have been personal computers. How else can you get advice from professionals like Keith Rollin and Leonard Rosenthal? Or get the real story from the employees at Apple, Microsoft, or Taligent? You couldn't talk to these folks by calling them up on the phone. That's the beauty of the net. It's the great equalizer.

get your battles back on track. Got a question? Find the right place to ask the question—then ask it. SmartFriends are more powerful than technical support. Able to leap taller problems in a single bound.

So you've decided to find a SmartFriend—one of those immortals who breathes code, a total Mac hacker—but you don't know where to start? No problem. Just follow these easy steps:

1. **Get online.** Now. Or risk being terminally unhip and hopeless.

2. **Hang out.** Frequent the popular places, both electronic and analog. Like in the old west, the only way to find a gunslinger is to drink in the saloons. Look for help online, but also at local user groups, universities, and computer stores (are there any left anymore?).

3. **Help others.** If someone has a question and you've got the answer, well, speak up already. That's the only way the Borg-like collective-consciousness of electronic communication can work.

Note

Although it's great to help out whenever you can, if six people have already answered a particular question, it would be truly annoying for you to add the same response. Be heads-up and see what messages were posted after each question before you waste network bandwidth. You're fellow e-denizens will thank you.

On CompuServe, real programmers spend their time in the Programmer's SIG. Visit this area and you'll be in the company of some of the best Mac hackers around.

On America Online, a good place to get general questions answered is in the Mac Operating System forum. Talk to AFAGene; he can help you, or guide you to one of his SmartFriends.

On the Internet, listen in on the comp.sys.mac. newsgroups. I especially like comp.sys.mac.comm due to the friendly people, most of whom seem quick to answer thorny communications and network questions (things I absolutely hate). The comp.sys.mac.programmer newsgroup is required reading for anyone who toils over Mac code. The best of the best hang out here; this is the end of the bar where Clint Eastwood's characters would sit if they happened to program Macs, which is a bit of a metaphorical stretch.

2

The Quest for Shareware

One hundred thousand years ago, our ancestors tried to find natural occurrences of fire, struggling to save and protect the valuable resource wherever they could find it. Like our ancestors following thunderstorms looking for lightning strikes, we stroll through the online service of our choice and collect shareware at our leisure. (Come to think of it, there's really no comparison at all. Sorry.)

All of the major online services mentioned earlier, as well as the Internet, offer immense libraries of shareware. It's from these libraries that I've pulled much of the contents of this book.

Folks have been posting shareware for a long, long time. There're lots out there. In the coming chapters, I'll show you what you can find and where to look. But don't just take my word for it. Get out there, root around, see what you can find. Think of a huge library with tall stacks filled with books: there's so much stuff, you can spend the rest of your

life just poking around. I'll show you the hot spots to check, but it's always more fun to discover things on your own. So go out and surf the net. It's very likely you'll find the shareware of your dreams.

Netsurfing USA

Here's where to go on the Internet to find all the really useful information any programmer could want:

Usenet Newsgroups

People post messages to these groups every hour of the day. Computer programmers looking for lively discussions about their language of choice may find the following groups interesting:

Note

Groups come and go. If you can't find one below, then surf the net and find it's equivalent.

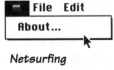

Netsurfing

(net-sər-fiŋ) *n: the sport of cruising the electronic online world*

comp.lang.c
comp.lang.c++
comp.forth
comp.forth.mac
comp.lisp
comp.lisp.mcl
comp.lang.pascal
comp.lang.smalltalk

Mac Programmers will especially like:

comp.sys.mac.programmer
This group is the nexus for net-based discussions between real live Mac programmers.

comp.sys.mac.databases

If you do anything with databases—4D, Filemaker Pro, Omnis, or Helix—you should definitely hang out here.

comp.sys.mac.comm

Use this newsgroup to get any of your communications questions answered—from "what kind of modem is best" to "how do I terminate a MacTCP connection?"

comp.sys.mac.oop.macapp3

comp.sys.mac.oop.tcl

Object-oriented programming has already become a standard of Macintosh programming. If you use one of these class libraries, then you should watch the traffic in these groups. I've had many a bug fixed by helpful posts here.

comp.sys.powerpc

To get the latest scoop on programming for the PowerPC chip, stick your nose in here every once in a while. It pays to keep current on new technology even if it doesn't affect you. It will someday soon.

comp.sys.newton.programmer

Programming for the Newton is a relatively new area, but there's more than enough traffic to keep this group interesting. If you're thinking about writing Newton apps, definitely check this out.

WAIS Servers

While newsgroups are great, there's no general way to look up past answers. If someone said anything three weeks ago about that printing bug you've encountered, you're just plum out of luck. WAIS (wide-area information search) will let you search an Internet-based database for certain topics. There are two good Mac databases:

Results! Why, man, I have gotten a lot of results. I know seven thousand things that won't work
—*Thomas A. Edison*

tcl.talk.src

The database stores the traffic from the tcl-talk mailing list. You can search for any word or combination of words. It's an awe-inspiring thing, for instance, to search for "Printing and bug" and see what comes up.

mac.FAQ.src

The frequently updated Mac FAQ (list of Frequently Asked Questions) is stored here. Thanks to WAIS, you can search through the whole thing (which is fairly large) and find the passage you need pronto.

The Shareware Tool Chest

The waters can be treacherous if you aren't prepared. You might find these tools useful while netsurfing.

- **ZTerm** This is the best shareware terminal emulation program available on the Mac. In fact, it's almost better than commercial programs costing four times as much. With it, you get scripting, on-screen PC-ANSI graphics, and Z-Modem transfers (which are a special kind of transfer that can resume where they were left off if you are interrupted, a truly cool feature).

- **StuffIt Expander** This workhorse should never be far from your desktop. Files you download will be compressed, so you can download them faster (and save bucks on the online charges). StuffIt Expander will decompress just about any kind of compressed file: StuffIt Lite, StuffIt Deluxe, AppleLink package files, and Compactor Pro files. Plus, it will de-binhex files that you collect from the Internet. The only file format it doesn't decompress is Disk Doubler.

- **StuffIt Lite** If you're going to be uploading files for the world to see, then you'll need to compress them first. StuffIt Lite is the shareware version of the popular StuffIt Deluxe program. It compresses files very quickly, and in the ongoing battle for world's best compressor, I think the StuffIt family has the edge (for the moment).

- **UnZip** If you connect with BBSs often or download files that come from MS-DOS machines, you'll need Unzip. The most commonly used compression program in the MS-DOS universe is PK Zip. Any Zip files you download (and it's easy to tell, since the name ends with .ZIP) will need to be decompressed with this program.

- **Disinfectant** A sad fact of the computer world is viruses. While the Mac hasn't had a real virus scare in a while, anyone who regularly downloads software from online services needs to be concerned about viruses. An online service is like a bathtub in a brothel: you never know what you'll catch. Disinfectant is a free program that will scan your hard disk (or a floppy, external drives, or even single files) for any known viruses. It also will install a system extension that scans continuously for virus-like activity. Use this program regularly, or one day you'll be sorry.

(For your convenience, and because I'm a really nice guy, I've loaded onto the disks that accompany this book the five programs just mentioned.)

Coming Up Next: Crash, Bam, Thank you, Man

Okay, we're nearly ready to head out into the dangerous online world. Check your disk for your online tools. Get them ready for the adventure ahead. Got your map? Then dig your trenches and set your trip-wires. This is war, people.

In the next chapter, we'll be covering first aid: what to do when your computer crashes. How do you recover? How do you prevent crashes from happening? Read Chapter 3 and take it to heart, that's what you do.

Trouble in Hacksville: When Good Macs Go Bad

Computers, because of their very nature, are extremely easy to render inoperative.
—William Powell, The Anarchist Cookbook

Computers crash. Any third-grade joystick jockey can tell you that. Crashes can occur with painful ease. It's not that computers are inherently unreliable—in fact, as far as their electrical components go, they're incredibly reliable. Ironic, eh?

So why does everyone fear crashing the system whenever they pick up the mouse? Software is the culprit, and lazy programmers deserve most of the blame. It's not impossible to make a program that almost never crashes, but it's a lot easier to make one that "only" crashes four or five times a day.

So, as a programmer striving for perfect code, you'll have to work defensively. Set up razor wire around your system folder. Place sandbags and machine-gun nests around your hard drive. Run sentry wires out to the memory. You get the idea—this is war.

You might find it strange that this entire chapter is about setting up rules to follow to avoid crashing, but programmers spend 80 percent of their time breaking all the rules. Ironic, right?

in this chapter, you'll find some simple strategies for keeping clear of crashes. No matter what kind of computer you have, there are some rules to keep in mind. I'll make it easy for you. Follow the rules: ☺. Don't follow the rules: ☹. Get the picture?

Note

This chapter, while chock full o' technical goodness, is meant for readers with a little less experience. While there's something in here for everybody, I'm certain most readers will gloss over it. That's okay. I would skip this chapter if I had just bought this book. Go ahead. You won't hurt my feelings. But someday you'll be back.

Dodging the Bullet

Psst, hey you, c'mere. Wanna know how to never, ever crash? There are some simple things you can do to make your computing life longer, fuller, and richer. Here are the basics:

- Use as few extensions (INITs, extensions, Cdevs, control panels, TSRs, whatever you call them) as possible.
- Add more RAM to your system.

That's all there is to it. I bet your glad you're reading this now and not *after* your computer crashed.

Extensions from Hell (and How to Deal with Them)

A guy I work with has three rows of extensions on his screen at startup. (And this guy has a 21-inch monitor!) He installs anything and everything he can get his hands on, and then he wonders (aloud) why his machine crashes so much. Well, duh!

It's easy to go extension crazy. Everyone has a spell of it at some point. Most of us grow out of it. Many others don't.

Because extensions are fun, crazy, zany, and sometimes even useful, it's a sad fact of life that to avoid crashes you have to use extensions sparingly. These days some of the coolest system software (QuickTime, QuickDraw GX, AppleScript) come as extensions. It's tough to pare down to the essentials.

Four steps to a better Mac

If your machine crashes regularly, follow these steps:

1. *Start your Mac while holding the* SHIFT *key down. (You knew this, right?)*

2. *Remove all your extensions. If you fit the profile, you've already got Startup Manager by Now Utilities or the shareware Extensions Manager (that comes on the disk with this book) or something similar. Use it.*

3. *One by one, return the extensions to your System Folder and then restart.*

4. *When you find the culprit, call the 800 number for the company that made it and complain for a long, long time.*

The following lists some extensions that are usually fail-safe—and some you're better off not using:

- More than likely, basic system-level components in your standard extension set from Apple are safe: QuickTime, AppleScript, and so forth. That's not to say these standard Apple extensions won't conflict with other software, but alone they almost never cause problems.

- Less common stuff from Apple, such as Plaintalk Speech Recognition, the Telephone Manager, or the Express Modem software, is generally safe but somewhat suspect. Apple even goes so far as to officially discourage use of some of its older and more esoteric extensions, such as the infamous Macintalk "speech synthesis" extension used before the release of the Quadra AVs. If you're having trouble, turn these off.

3

- Third-party extensions are always suspect unless you've run them for a long time and know them to be safe. Based on my experience, products from Now Software, Fifth Generation Systems, and Aladdin Software tend to be bulletproof. But many other smaller software shops have looser beta-test procedures and smaller test groups, and therefore can't predict and prevent every problem. Use the remove-restart method given earlier to catch conflicts.

Mo' Memory

Like money, compact discs, and Hummel figurines, when it comes to memory, you can never have too much. Memory (RAM, in this instance) is the good stuff you need. Every program you run uses it. Low-memory conditions can lead to system crashes.

Most system crashes are caused by lazy programmers who don't do their homework. Low-memory conditions are just the stresses that bring structural faults into the light.

If you're a programmer and you don't check MemError (or for a nil handle) after every allocation, you're guilty. (Hey, relax, I'm just as guilty as anyone. We're all pretty lazy when we can get away with it.)

If you've forced yourself to cut back on extensions, but still have enough to choke your system memory partition, the next best thing is to add lots o' RAM. If you run lots and lots of extensions, they'll chew up a significant portion of your system memory, and your applications will feel the squeeze. Buy as much RAM as you can. These days 8 megabytes (MB) is the minimum, 16 MB is reasonable, and 32 MB is probably more than most people need.

Programmers need plenty of RAM—for the compilers, editors, debuggers, and so forth that they'll want to run. Don't skimp on RAM. No other factor—not even processor speed—so directly affects your user experience.

ram is pretty much a commodity these days, like orange juice or pork bellies. No one prints prices in magazines or books anymore: you have to call and get the price du jour, which can fluctuate wildly from yesterday's or tomorrow's price. When a Japanese RAM glue factory caught fire in 1993, RAM prices went through the roof for several months. The opportunity to gouge was apparently too great to resist.

watch

the prices for a while and ask a SmartFriend to make sure you're not getting juked. Buy only RAM that has a lifetime warranty. Some day you'll be glad you did. Also, buy RAM from established companies. Most will match the lower prices from the Joe's House O' RAM-type joints, and they'll probably be around a lot longer to honor their warranties. I usually buy RAM from these good fellas:

Tech Works   1-(800)-278-7090

Peripheral Outlet   1-(800)-256-6581

They have overnight service, great manuals and tech support, and a lifetime guarantee. I have been buying RAM from both of them for years, and I don't see any reason to switch to anyone else. (And no, they didn't give me a freebie in exchange for this plug.)

Virtually Speaking

Virtual memory is a control panel feature that takes a portion of your hard disk and pretends it's actually RAM. This way, you can have as much "RAM" as you have free space on your hard drive. (Don't confuse virtual memory—or virtual RAM—with a RAM disk, which creates a "virtual hard disk" out of available RAM memory.)

I use virtual memory, but know very few other people who do. Virtual memory slows the computer down, since it has to swap information from RAM to the hard drive and vice versa. Hard drive access takes much longer than RAM access, which means all of your programs run more slowly.

and

some programs can't truck with virtual memory. Adobe Photoshop uses its own virtual memory scheme, which confuses your system's virtual memory. Many CD-ROM games try to improve their speed by loading as much data into RAM as possible; since virtual

3

memory isn't really RAM, they end up being slower than they would have been.

You'll need to give up a chunk of your hard drive to make virtual memory work. If you turn on 32 MB of virtual memory on your 8 MB Mac, you'll need to have 24 MB of disk space free. It's a trade-off: (virtually) more RAM in exchange for some hard disk space. If you're tight on disk space, you may not be able to swing it.

All that said, I like using virtual memory. I have 16 MB of RAM on my computer, and 60 MB of virtual "RAM" memory. Most everything I run fits in RAM, and there's very little swapping. But whenever I do run a program that kicks me over the 16 MB limit, virtual memory lets me avoid the annoying "Not enough memory" dialogs and I don't have to dig through menus for a program to close.

Crawl to the Mirage

If you're a programmer, you'll probably be crashing more often than not. Here's a tip I use to keep from crashing my hard drive: use a RAM disk.

Crash! Bam! Boom!

There's a difference between crashing your computer and crashing your hard drive. Your computer crashes because it is forced to execute some instruction it logically can't, such as "divide by zero" (which results in infinity, for those of us who are mathematically challenged—don't feel bad, I had to look it up myself). The result is you restart your computer and things are more or less as they were before the crash, except for some lost or scrambled data.

Hard disk crashes are caused by a corruption of some data on your hard drive, usually in the directory portion of the disk that lists where all of the files are located, or sometimes in the section of the disk that informs the computer how to start itself (called the boot blocks). The result is your Mac won't boot up properly, or perhaps won't boot at all.

Crashing your computer can crash your hard drive, especially during disk operations. Recommendation: back up early and often.

Since a RAM disk simulates a real disk in memory, anything that happens to it won't affect your hard drive. If you have enough RAM, you can even load your entire system on it and run the entire computer from it.

this way, when you crash (or trash the system file, or whatever) it happens to the RAM disk, not (you hope) your hard disk. And (the best part) if you totally, completely, absolutely screw up everything in the active system, you can just reboot from the hard drive and start over.

Another great benefit: there's no faster way to run your Mac than from a RAM disk. It's amazingly fast. Your compile and link times will be much faster, resources get copied into the application with great alacrity, and if you need to do a global search, it's done in mere seconds.

Try it; you'll like it. Of course, this means you'll need more RAM again. Ironic, no? (Honestly, I do not work for the RAM cartel...yet. It's just one of the things you need to bite the bullet and buy.)

Yin vs. Yang

A client of mine, a guy at a large firm, claimed his Mac was running slow. I dropped by to take a look. He was low on RAM, so he did the obvious thing: he turned on virtual memory. And then, since he felt his Mac was still slow, he set up a RAM disk.

Virtual memory fakes the system into thinking that part of the hard disk is system memory. And a RAM disk fakes the system into thinking that part of the system RAM is actually a hard disk. So in the end, not only did this guy gain nothing, he slowed things down substantially thanks to his yin vs. yang virtual memory and RAM disk programs.

Moral of the story: think. (You know that's IBM's corporate slogan: Think! More irony.) Steve Jobs's fantasy about an appliance computer has failed to materialize. Sadly, you must learn a few basic facts about how these things work. There's just no other way to happily use a computer.

3

Patching Traps and Other Scary Stuff

And now for the moment you've been waiting for: techno-babble. Hang onto your hats! Kids, check with you parents first!

When an application calls upon the system to do something—say, draw a rectangle—the program uses what's known as a trap. It's called this because of the mechanism behind the scenes: when the system routine is called, an error condition is generated; the 680x0 chip actually traps the error code and transfers control to a routine, pulled from a big ol' list of routines, called the "trap dispatch table."

Since there is a table of traps and their addresses in ROM memory, it's not too hard to change the trap table so that some code you've written can be executed instead of the ROM code. In fact, that's what nearly all extensions or INITs do; they "patch the traps," so that they (the INITs) get run instead of a system trap, and then they (the INITs again) call the system's code as the last thing they do.

if this seems complicated, don't worry: all you really need to know is that the system has a list of all the routines it calls to do any work, and you can replace those routines with one of your own. Whenever you install an extension or a control panel, at some level it's what they do.

This explains why many INITs or extensions can conflict with each other. Say, for instance, you install two extensions that patch the FrameRect procedure inside the ROM. Which one is run? The last one to load. What happens to the first one? It's stranded deep in hyperspace. What if it depends on code in that routine? Crash city, most likely.

The Moral of the Story

The moral: test your shareware! Not just on your own machine, but on as many different Macs as you can. If you can't do it, ask around online—you're sure to dig up some warm bodies who are always willing to test whatever's new. (There is a class of people who only want software that no one else has. Find these people and exploit them mercilessly.) Your end users will thank you. I will thank you. Personally, if I must.

Passing the test

A complete test suite would include running your program on every different processor Apple ever shipped:

- Mac Plus, Mac SE, Mac Portable, or PowerBook 100 (68000 chip)

- Mac II, Mac LC (68020 chip)

- Mac SE/30, Mac IIsi, Mac IIci (68030 chip)

- Quadra 700, Quadra 950, Quadra 605, and so on

- Power Macintosh 6100, 7100, 8100, as well as the PowerPC PDS upgrade card (PowerPC 601 chip)

Many people will skimp on the 68000 and the 68020. And that's too bad, because there are many simple-to-stumble-upon yet easy-to-fix crashes on the 68000.

the art of testing software deserves a book in its own right. Suffice it to say, you need to test every function in your program under every environment. The number of variables quickly becomes staggering, and too many programmers become overwhelmed by the magnitude of this step and do their testing in the marketplace, i.e. by releasing untested shareware to the world. While this has worked for some, you can very possibly earn a really bad name in the shareware market if things go wrong with your release.

Your average shareware jockey has a line like this in his or her ReadMe file "I wrote this Cdev. It runs on my IIcx, but not on my sister's Performa or my buddy's Quadra. Try it out on your system. It's pretty cool." At best, this attitude is unprofessional; at worst, it's criminal. Test that shareware! You'll be glad you did.

Macsbug, the Wonder Drug

A debugger is a program that you use to help squash the bugs in your own programs. Debuggers patch into the system at the lowest level, and provide a way for you to step through each machine language instruction of your program, or even Apple's ROM code.

Of course, you'll need to understand at least a little machine language to get by in the debugger. The more you know, the more you can get out of it. But even if you know nothing about machine language, you can do amazing things with a debugger installed.

if you're an official Macintosh developer, or you hang with the right user-group crowds, or you scour net-land, you can get a copy of Macsbug, Apple's official debugger for the Macintosh. Macsbug is a powerful tool—indeed we'll spend much time discussing it in later chapters—but even for simple crashes, it can be immensely helpful.

In the end, it's tools like Macsbug that separate us—the programmers, hackers, and overall smart users—from other Mac fanatics. We use a debugger. People who don't are sheep who have lost their way. They see the bomb icon 50 times a day and peck at the INTERRUPT button and slap around at the

COMMAND-OPTION-ESCAPE combo like a trout tossed onto a Georgia parking lot on the Fourth of July. We just install Macsbug, tap a couple of keys, and keep on trucking.

Macsbug Sources

Macsbug is a product from Apple. You can purchase it from APDA (800-282-2732 US, 716-71-6555 for non-American callers). Since they sell it, it's not generally available on online services or BBSs. Many user groups have it and can provide it to you free of cost.

Also, check the Apple Developer CD-ROMs (which Apple sends to you if you're an official developer, in which case you're not bothering to read this sidebar). To become an official Apple developer, call the Developer Support Center at -(408)-974-4897 or send them e-mail at devsupport@applelink.apple.com.

Or check with your favorite SmartFriend.

3

When your Mac crashes, it will attempt to use the debugger to inform you of the crash. Under really serious circumstances, even this won't work: you may find your mouse frozen, immobile, pathetically trapped. Don't panic. Try pressing the INTERRUPT button on your computer. Sometimes you'll get the debugger; other times, you'll be just as stuck as you were before. If this happens, your only recourse is to reboot. (The other switch—Restart—is a bang-up way to get this done.)

In the Trenches with Macsbug, Part I

Once you've crashed, you'll want to recover. These commands can get you back on your feet. Many people suspect that when you crash with Macsbug, recovery is much more successful. People report that when using Macsbug with the commands given next, the dreaded "hard reboot" appears onscreen far less often. I can't imagine why this would be—I think our brains are playing tricks on us. But it sure seems that Macsbug helps.

when

your computer presents the Macsbug screen, type them in on the command line. You can type "?" in Macsbug for a full list of commands (and there are many) so I'll list just the most useful ones here:

ES Exit to Shell (which takes you back to the desktop).

EA Exit to Application (which never works)

Find out the subtle points over which it is easy to prevail, attack what can be overcome, do not attack what cannot be overcome.

—Sun Tzu

RB Reboot the Mac. This is the same as pressing the RESET button on your Mac's programmer's switch.

RS Restart the Macintosh; this is the same as selecting RESTART from the Finder's "Special" menu. Use this with caution, however. RESTART will flush the disk cache—the area of memory where recent changes to the disk are stored. If you've crashed, you may have hosed this cache. If you write a hosed cache out to the disk, you've just corrupted the thing. If all this scares you, use RB instead of RS. (For the record, I use RS and have never had a problem.)

Dissecting crashes is interesting and fun. It also can get you serious respect on tech-support phone lines (saying things like "Yeah, your program crashed with a zero divide in DrawNextWord" can really impress bored tech support drones).

on

the flip side, a crash is less fun to dissect if it's your own program that crashed. Usually there's a lot of work involved in finding out what happened; it's not uncommon for a Mac crash to occur far from the offensive line of code. Debugging is its own art, and it's best covered by itself. We'll talk more about debuggers in Chapter 8. Also check out the Torah of Mac debugging guides, *How To Write Macintosh Software* by Scott Knaster (Reading, MA: Addison Wesley, 1992). If you don't own that book yet, I feel your shame. Now go buy it.

When you write shareware, it's a good idea to ask users who have Macsbug to give you more information when they crash. For instance, if you build your application with Debugger Names on, anyone with Macsbug can trace your code to see exactly where the crash occurred. This helps immensely in solving a problem your user is having from a long way away. Also, you can instruct your users to do a stack crawl, so you can see all of the procedures and functions called up until the crash.

In the Trenches with Macsbug, Part II

If you're a programmer, here's a few Macsbug commands to get you by:

SC Stack Crawl will list all of the procedures and functions that have been called up until the point of the crash, so you can track where your program has been. It doesn't always work; it's easy to hose the data structures that store this information. Try "SC7" if SC doesn't help.

HT Heap Total will show you the amount of free memory in your program's partition. It also shows how many blocks are locked, purgeable, or both.

HD Heap Display shows you the actual blocks on memory in the heap. You can type "HD PICT" to see all of the pictures loaded from resources, or "HD SND" to see all of the sounds, for instance.

Tip

A good way to cause a sneaky crash is to dispose of a NIL handle. Or, even worse, you might access a handle after it's been disposed of. But both of these are pretty easy to avoid. Just stick this code into your program:

```
procedure MyDisposeHandle(var h : univ Handle);
var
    tempH: Handle;
begin
tempH := h;
if (tempH<> nil) then begin
    h := nil;
    DisposeHandle(tempH);
end;
```

*That's Think Pascal, for those you of wondering. C
programmers, you'll just have to translate. Anyway, this
routine dodges the bullet by only disposing of a handle if it's
not nil; also, it sets the handle to nil after it disposes of it, so
that you won't be tempted to access memory that you no
longer own. Use it every time, and you'll be wiser and happier.
(More wisdom of this sort can be found on the Apple
Developer CD-ROMs, in the pages of MacTech Magazine, and
from your favorite SmartFriend.)*

Prevention Is the Cure

The best way to recover from a crash is to prepare ahead
of time.

- Set up an external disk (a removable Syquest cartridge,
  an external hard disk, whatever) with a copy of your
  System Folder and a drive repair utility. Even if you just
  take a 20 MB hard drive and stick a minimal System
  Folder on it, or just use a floppy disk with the System
  and Finder on it, you'll be able to boot the computer.

- If you have a hard disk utility program, such as the
  popular Norton Utilities (from Symantec), or the equally
  good Public Utilities (from Fifth Generation Systems),
  put it on the disk too. If you don't, put a copy of Apple's
  Disk First Aid on it. If that's all you do, it's better than
  sending your hard disk to DiskSavers at $180 an hour
  for data recovery.

- I recommend Norton and Public Utilities because each
  one can automatically create an emergency startup disk
  tailored for your computer, including all of the Enabler
  files you'll need.

- Back up, back up, back up. I know I sound like your
  mother. Do it now, scumbag! I know no one likes to do it,
  and God knows I do it rarely enough, but it's the only
  way to be sure. It's the only way to be safe. Back up your
  hard disk at least every week, and more often if you can.

Crash and Burn

So you've finally done it. You've crashed the whole dang thing. Your computer won't even boot anymore. Don't feel bad, we've all done it. It's a fact of computing life. Dry your eyes and reach for these floppies.

if you followed the instructions given earlier, you're eating pork with a fork. Just use your special Emergency Disk and let it work its magic.

These kinds of programs can usually recover from any common crash, and many uncommon ones. In fact, I've never had a crash where Public Utilities couldn't save my butt.

Too cheap to buy a hard disk utility? There's still hope. Boot your computer with the "Disk Tools" floppy that comes with every Mac.

3

Tip

If you have a Performa, you didn't get disks when you bought your computer. You were supposed to make some from disk images on the hard disk, first thing after you got home. You did make those floppies, didn't you?

Disk Tools should boot your computer, and it also should let you run a program called Disk First Aid. (It's a good idea to make a copy of the Disk Tools disk and store it in a cool, dry place.) Disk First Aid will check for common problems—bad blocks in the directory sectors, inconsistencies in the file control blocks, and so forth,

In the end, if the utilities fail you, you'll need to boot from a floppy or a CD and reformat your hard drive. Ugly and messy, I know, but usually necessary. I really, really hope you're reading this while your computer is safe and sound. If it is, great. Put this book down and go back up your hard drive. This book will wait.

Any programmer worth his or her salt will totally screw up a hard drive at some point. You know it's going to happen.

Prepare for it. Laugh at it when it happens. You're safe.
You're backed up.

Coming Up Next:
Shareware-at-Large

Starting with the next chapter, we'll get into reviews of
actual products you can use to make life easier. Some
all-time shareware favorites, along with a few forgotten
gems and even an unheralded masterpiece or two, await just
pages ahead. Don't be shy. Turn that page.

Altering Reality: Utilities for a Better Life

Utilities for a Better Life

Edit	
Cut	⌘H
Quote	⌘Q
Copy	⌘C

Certain drugs affect the mind and allow the individual, for the first time, to see the world freely, without enforced values and rituals. For the first time the person can see clearly the real inequities and the farcical absurdities.
—William Powell, The Anarchist Cookbook

Good shareware utilities are to hackers what LSD was to hippies: both alter the user's perception of the world. In this chapter, and those that follow, we're going to take an in-depth look at dozens of the very best available hacks for programmers. These aren't just for fun and games: this shareware can change your work habits (and maybe even your life) for the better.

There are many good Mac utility packages out there. Before I discuss my favorite shareware offerings, I first want to cover one commercial package that I find invaluable, and that you might consider using also. The Now Utilities package, from Now Software, is available from your favorite retail or mail-order outlet. I recommend the Now Utilities because they are useful and stable. Now Software has been through several versions of the Now Utilities package, which is compatible with most utilities you're likely to use. Also, I haven't come across a single shareware offering (or suite of shareware programs) that provides so much functionality. Many come close, but none provides so much power and flexibility. Consider these Now Utilities benefits:

- SuperBoomerang, part of Now Utilities, makes the task of finding and using files much, much easier. Whenever you reach an Open dialog box (that's an SFGetFile to you programmers), a series of pop-up menus lets you quickly switch to your favorite folders. Using SuperBoomerang, you can easily jump between the directories that contain your source code, your class libraries, the standard interfaces, and so on.

- You also can create folders as you're saving a file, a feature that Apple should have added to the Save As dialog box long ago. And you can search for a file from the Open dialog box; so even if you have no idea where you put that durn source code file, you can locate and open it in a flash.

- NowMenus adds hierarchical menus to the items under the Apple menu. So if you place aliases to folders in your Apple Menu Items folder, you'll be able to get to any file that is in that directory from the Apple menu.

- There are several good shareware alternatives to NowMenus (one that I've used is MenuChoice), but NowMenus has a few other features that its shareware competitors can't match. NowMenus lets you create keyboard shortcuts for virtually any menu choice. Think Pascal doesn't have a key equivalent for the Build Application menu option? No problem! NowMenus will let you set one.

- Imagine the standard Mac Scrapbook on a strict diet of red meat and rye whiskey and you get a pretty good idea of what NowScrapbook is like. It has a scrollable table of contents (each item can be given a descriptive name), so finding that TIFF file you pasted in two weeks ago isn't a laborious process. You also can view thumbnail-sized images of all items in the scrapbook, which is very handy if you use lots of pictures. And speaking of pictures, you can edit them with the clipboard editor it provides.

Tip

I keep multiple NowScrapbook files, each with a different kind of content. For example, as I come across cool and useful source code fragments online or on the Internet, I clip them and store them in a NowScrapbook file. I keep a separate file for each kind of code—one file for QuickDraw stuff, another for CDEV samples, and so on.

You don't get dirty in banks. You go home with neckties on and not one piece of dirt on your clothes.

—John Fay

Don't think I'm a traitor to the shareware cause. Most aspects of Now Utilities started life as shareware, and like many people I got hooked on this stuff early. When it went commercial, I had to buy it—how else could I get the latest features and bug fixes?

This is sort of like liking the band REM. I liked REM when every album held indecipherable gibberish. When the band got big, some huge corporation forced the group to became listenable. It seems all the other old fans got on the band's case for "going commercial". Hey, at least now you can hear what they're saying! Is that so bad? It's the same with Now Utilities. I love SuperBoomerang even more now, since the bugs get fixed regularly!

Software licenses suck

Most software comes shrink-wrapped with an annoying little sticker on the package that says, "This software is the property of the huge MicroStuff conglomerate. You, unworthy peon, are only licensing it. You're lucky we even let you do that. If you have a problem with it, stick it in your ear."

A long time ago, in a galaxy far, far away, this was a good thing for everyone. If you wrote an incredible accounting application (an oxymoron, I realize) for some client, it was best to license it. Licensing was good for programmers, because it meant they owned their code and it wasn't a work for hire, so they could sell it again and again. Licensing was good for the client who bought it, because the programmers would be tied to them via the license agreement and couldn't get away with lousy, buggy software.

4

Of course licensing today has different connotations. MicroStuff licenses the software to you, and you live with the buggy software you (and millions of other schmucks) paid for but do not own. Think about it: we as Americans have given MicroStuff billions of dollars. MicroStuff has given us nothing in return, except the right to use their buggy software until they decide to terminate the agreement.

When the midwest was flooded, many people lost master floppy disks of their software. One company in particular (which shall remain nameless, but it sells a popular desktop publishing application) refused to replace the master disks. Even though these folks were registered users, and were in the company's database of legit owners, they were refused new master disks. "Pony up the bucks for a new copy," the company said. Some users even offered to send in blank floppies but the company refused to help these folks as well.

This sucks. Licensing agreements are laughable, insulting, and (if there was any justice in this world) indefensible in court. If you're a programmer, avoid the temptation to pay some slick lawyer thousands of dollars to write one. Follow the lead of folks like DeltaTau Software, who avoid insulting your intelligence by actually selling, not licensing, the software to you.

The Gloves Come Off

The rest of this chapter lists useful programs from around the shareware universe. I've scanned the world over. I've asked around on the Internet. And this is it: the top shareware for programmers and hackers.

Based on the things I see online, most Mac programmers don't know about many of the following hacks. That's too bad—your efforts can be aided immeasurably by applying a specific hack at the right time.

Get some leverage from the folks who've done the hard work for you. These are things that can make your programming life easier. Your code will fly off your fingertips. Debugging time will whiz by. Life gets good.

Hack Facts

```
AppDisk
APPL
Version1.5
Mark Adams
1215 Research Blvd. #2036
Austin, TX 78759
$15
```

AppDisk is a RAM disk utility. (What's a RAM disk? See chapter 3.) Sure, you could just use Apple's built-in RAM disk, which you control from the Memory control panel, but AppDisk has several nice features that the control panel lacks.

ppDisk is implemented as an application. To use it, just double-click it. A new disk icon will appear on your desktop. To change the amount of memory the disk is using, simply change the application's memory size in the "Get Info" box in the Finder.

AppDisk can save the RAM disk contents when you shut down, or it can be set to save every few minutes (if you're as anal as I am, you'll like this). This information is saved in the data fork of the application, so there are no rogue or invisible files hanging around your hard disk just to keep your RAM disk contents.

Tip

When using Think Pascal or C, you can substantially speed up your program build cycle by placing the project, source code, and resource files on a RAM disk.

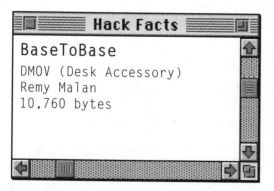

Hack Facts

```
BaseToBase
DMOV (Desk Accessory)
Remy Malan
10,760 bytes
```

Back in the old days, hackers worth their salt could not only count in hexadecimal, but add, subtract, multiply, and divide in it as well. Nowadays, most hackers are like me: I'd love to learn how, but since I got cable, who has the time?

4

Hexadecimal rock

The hexadecimal system is, in lay terms, another way of counting things. In mathematician's terms, hexadecimal is a base 16 numbering system. When you count on your fingers, that's base 10. (Base 20 if you use your toes.) In hexadecimal you count like this: 1,2,3,4,5,6,7,8,9,A,B,C,D,E,F,10,11,12,13, 14,15,16,17,18,19,1A,1B,1C,1D,1E,1F,20. And so on. Hex numbers are used extensively in low-level programming and debugging.

That's why BaseToBase has a hallowed spot in my Apple Menu Items folder. I'd much rather watch ten hours of mindless TV than learn a valuable skill that could make me a more productive person.

BaseToBase will convert numbers from decimal to hex, octal, and binary (see Figure 4-1). You can change on the fly—for instance, you can do some calculations in decimal, and then switch to hex to see the result. This is very handy for tracking down the location of a bitmap in Macsbug.

a l s o handy are the logical functions: and, not, or, nor, xor. If you've ever wondered why your mask bits weren't working right, you probably needed something like this.

I also had one shareware tester laud the benefits of BaseToBase as an aid for working with his digital sampling keyboard.

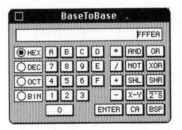

Figure 4-1. *FFFEA isn't the Federal Fund For Exterminating Animals, though there is a nice ring to it. It's simply the number 1,048,554*

Although this guy spent way too many hours sampling sounds from the Kennedy assassination and World Championship Wrestling, he swears BaseToBase made it easier.

Wonder of wonders: this program is a desk accessory. I've had it since 1986. And it still works today on my Quadra. They don't lie when they tell you to follow Apple's programming guidelines!

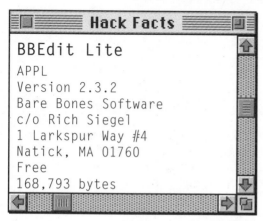

```
======= Hack Facts =======
BBEdit Lite
APPL
Version 2.3.2
Bare Bones Software
c/o Rich Siegel
1 Larkspur Way #4
Natick, MA 01760
Free
168,793 bytes
```

While Apple provides a simple program for editing text, it doesn't have any of the features a programmer needs. It doesn't open files larger than 32K. It doesn't even open more than one file at a time.

BBEdit Lite is an "industrial-strength" text editor, made for people who use really long text documents—not just programmers, but also engineers, mathematicians, and others who need to view huge text files as shown in Figure 4-2.

BBEdit is not a word processor—it offers very little flexibility in terms of fonts, text sizes, and so forth. That's not what it's about. BBEdit Lite was made to munch text files as quickly and painlessly as possible.

If your system has sufficient memory, there's no limit to the number of file windows you can have open. There's no limit to the length of a file. BBEdit Lite was designed for serious text editing.

These are just some of the features BBEdit Lite gives you:

- The ability to search all of the files in a folder for a word or phrase, even if the files aren't BBEdit Lite files, or aren't even text files. Search and replace is easy--and even the difficult-to-grok Grep search is an easy-to-use option.

```
/* the drawing routine goes in here */
void do_blackout(time)
long time; /* you can change the parameter to be
{
    /*
        YOUR CODE GOES IN HERE
    */

    ShowWindow(bigWindow);
    OffsetRect(&r,1,1);
    if (whichFrame == Frame1)
        whichFrame = Frame2;
    else whichFrame = Frame1;

    DrawPicture(whichFrame,&r);
//  DrawPicture(Frame2,&r);
    return;
}

/* look through the event queue (low-mem global)
int any_events(void)
```

Figure 4-2. *BBEdit tells you the date and time you last saved the document at the top of the window, so you can always remember exactly how much of a lifeless troll you've become*

- A "Twiddle" command, which can rearrange two switched characters in a typo.

- Parenthesis balancing, so you don't have to sit around and count how many you've typed.

- Some cool extensions that make commenting out a section of code a breeze. Programmers can extend BBEdit Lite using code resources they write themselves.

Tip

There is a commercial version of BBEdit, the features of which are far too numerous to list here. Suffice it to say that if you like BBEdit Lite, you'll love the commercial BBEdit. And even though it's commercial software, it's reasonably priced like shareware. Contact Rich Siegel at the above address for more information.

You can use it to edit your C or C++ files in conjunction with something like the Think Project Manager, although if you're

Figure 4-3.   *BBEdit Lite can open huge text files, in this case Joseph Conrad's **Heart of Darkness***

going to use it as your only programming editor, I would recommend purchasing the commercial version, which knows how to read Think Project Manager and Code Warrior project files.

But even if you're not, I recommend BBEdit Lite for anyone who telecommunicates. The Internet is full of huge text files. As shown in Figure 4-3, BBEdit Lite's the best way to tame them. And you can't beat the price.

A common frustration for Mac programmers, aside from the fact that *Star Trek* comes on but once a day, is that file icons never seem to show up when you make a new program.

What happens is that the Finder's invisible Desktop file is not being updated; the Finder really has no way of knowing that you've just compiled and built your masterpiece, and so it doesn't load your program's special icon (which you doubtless spent far more hours futzing with than you ever would have spent programming) into the Desktop file.

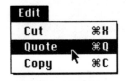

Fears for security really do louse up the free flow of information.
—Cliff Stoll

A simple way to remedy this is to rebuild the Desktop file, which you can do by holding down the COMMAND and OPTION keys as you reboot or by using a program such as File Buddy. However, if you've got a big hard drive (and who doesn't these days) this can take a very long time.

BNDL Banger solves this problem by cleverly inserting your program's special icon directly into the Desktop file. It's a messy hack that may not survive in future System versions, but so what? It works great for now. You still need to reboot, but generally that doesn't take nearly as long as rebuilding the Desktop file.

For the measly seven bucks he's asking, Tim will send you BNDL Banger Pro, which has additional features and the source code. (Remember, source code is Good.)

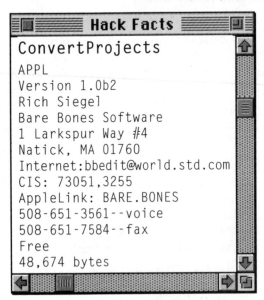

Hack Facts

ConvertProjects

APPL
Version 1.0b2
Rich Siegel
Bare Bones Software
1 Larkspur Way #4
Natick, MA 01760
Internet:bbedit@world.std.com
CIS: 73051,3255
AppleLink: BARE.BONES
508-651-3561--voice
508-651-7584--fax
Free
48,674 bytes

This wholesome American beauty converts Think Pascal and C project files to work with the new Code Warrior development environment. Code Warrior exploded onto the scene in early 1994 with the only compiler for PowerPC chips that actually worked on Macs. Before that, you had to compile PowerPC programs on an IBM RS/600workstation. (Gag, vomit, puke.)

Of course, Code Warrior has lost that PPC edge, but it still has a cool environment (despite the interface atrocity of toolbars). Gregory Dow (of the original Think Class Library fame) wrote the fantastic class library. It compiles both C and Pascal under the same umbrella, even for the same project, so you can use either code as you go.

ConvertProjects will take a project file for the Think Project Manager and convert it into a project file for the Code Warrior. If you decide to take the Code Warrior plunge, this will make your entry as smooth and splash-free as possible. Just drag your project file onto ConvertProjects and let go.

Note

One slap on the wrist for ConvertProjects is that it requires the Think Project Manager to operate. This is a pain. Not everyone who needs to convert projects has Think Project Manager. For instance, I just bought Code Warrior, and never bothered to update my Think C to version 6, which means ConvertProjects doesn't work for me.

```
        Hack Facts
CodeSucker
Version 1.02
Michael van Kleef
Flat 5, 4 St. Quintin Ave.
London, W106NU, England
$1
```

CodeSucker, as you can surmise from its name, sucks code resources (or any other resource) from running programs. You can save these sucked resources to disk, to examine at your leisure. As one of my Internet contacts put it, CodeSucker is the program I always wanted to write.

Figure 4-4 shows proof of wasted RAM: Why does my Quadras System use a driver that powers a PowerBook's backlight? Some Apple engineering whiz kid was asleep at the keys. CodeSucker is great for this kind of snooping. Note the two lists in Figure 4-4: one lists resource types and the other lists individual resources. By selecting a resource type and then any one resource, you can save the resource to disk

Resource Types	ID#	name	size
ADBS AINI	−16519	.MNP	22006
ALRT BNDL	−16517	.LTM	13968
CDEF CNTL	−16511	.Backlight	4304
CURS DITL	−16499	.AppleSound...	3764
DLOG DRVR	2	.Print	410
DSAT FKEY	9	.MPP	4920
FMTR FOND	10	.ATP	4214
FONT FREF	40	.XPP	3412
FRSV FRev			
GLNM GLOB			

CodeSucker v1.02 Rsrc File : System

Help | Quit | File ▼ | Save ▼

Figure 4-4. *Using CodeSucker to find examples of wasted RAM*

using the Save menu. The File menu will let you switch to any open resource file (although this did crash me when I switched to font files under System 7).

This provides a neat way of exploring the inner contents of programs you buy. It's also good for examining and debugging your own programs as they run. For instance, I wrote a program that keeps its current data in a resource handle; with CodeSucker, I could save these resources before I had a crash to examine their contents.

Michael van Kleef, the author, points out that this is a great way to save readable copies of compressed or encrypted resources. Since all resources are compressed by the resource manager when the resource is read into memory, when you suck a resource out of memory, you can be sure it's decompressed. And some programs (games, mostly) use encryption algorithms to hide their resources. CodeSucker slides around this otherwise impenetrable wall.

Super geeky bonus: Michael included the source code for this FKEY. It's in Pascal (yes!) and you can read through the files for a quick tutorial in writing FKEYs or using the List Manager or pop-up menus. This (like all source code) is essential reading if you're just starting out.

This FKEY—author unknown, please send me mail if it's you!—copies the RGB values of any color to the clipboard.

Activating the FKEY presents you with a standard color wheel. You choose the color you want, and the correct red, green, and blue values are pasted onto the clipboard.

This is really handy when you're programming at a fast clip and don't want to waste time switching into Photoshop or whatever.

You just hit your COPYRGB key to paste the resulting RGB values into your program. FKEY is great for anyone who programs using Color QuickDraw and QuickDraw GX.

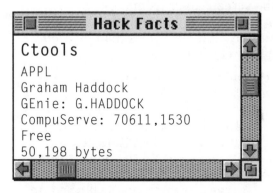

Hack Facts

```
Ctools
APPL
Graham Haddock
GEnie: G.HADDOCK
CompuServe: 70611,1530
Free
50,198 bytes
```

I found this program on the Internet when I needed to convert a bunch of C routines into Pascal, which is only one of its many tricks. Here are just a few examples of what this program can do:

- Format C source code
- Convert Pascal source into C source
- Check a C file for balancing { and }, as well as correct usage of = versus = =
- List the program flow for any C file
- Give variable and function cross-referencing

Since it uses standard TextEdit in its window, CTools can't handle files larger than 32K. The author says in the readme file, "Of course, you are never supposed to let your C source files get that long anyway." Yeah, right. Earth to Graham! Welcome to reality, bud.

It does everything adequately, and some things poorly. The Pascal to C converter requires quite a bit of hand-tuning. Luckily, a dialog box warns you of the kind of things to look for while hand-tuning, but you can't print or save these instructions. The Source code formatter didn't do much in the way of formatting. However, it did provide a very effective way to crash into the debugger.

Get it and try it if you think you'll need it but in the end you may decide (like me) just to chuck it and do it yourself. It's a wonderful idea—a bunch of handy source code massagers in a convenient package. It may be useful in certain circumstances. Unfortunately, it doesn't live up to its potential.

4

```
Hack Facts

DarkSide of the Mac
APPL
Version 3.2
Tom Dowdy
1610 Kamsack Dr.
Sunnyvale, CA 94087
$15
40,551 bytes
```

I'm gonna go out on a limb and say that the single program that best defines the totality of Macness is...After Dark, the screen saver from Berkeley Systems. I think more Macs have been sold by flying toasters than by, well, definitely flying helocars.

Screen savers, as a software genre, were born from the fear of a single static image burning permanently into the phosphors on your monitor (think of all those green monitors at your local library). But, in the quest for the coolest moving images to keep the phosphors from burning forever, programmers churned out some of the most creative Mac code yet.

But as much as I love it, After Dark is not perfect. Being an extension, it sometimes conflicts with other programs. Also, it tends to crash. Sometimes it crashes a lot.

Enter DarkSide of the Mac. DarkSide provides all of the fun, wit, and irreverence of After Dark, without the risk. I like DarkSide for two reasons: it's an application, and therefore it's a simple conceptual unit; you don't have to worry about where to put it or how to use it.

Also, it crashes much less frequently than After Dark. And in those rare instances when it does crash, it just quits to the Finder, leaving all of your other programs intact. Since After Dark loads into the system heap, odds are it will trash the system heap when it crashes.

True, the art used in DarkSide is not as professional as the art featured in After Dark. And while DarkSide imitates many

After Dark modules, you'll never be fooled into thinking one is the other based on speed and looks alone. But since switching to DarkSide, I've crashed a whole lot less, and that's all I need to know.

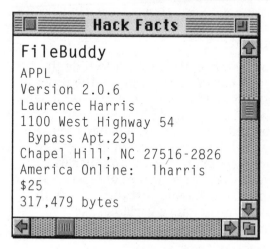

Hack Facts

FileBuddy
APPL
Version 2.0.6
Laurence Harris
1100 West Highway 54
 Bypass Apt.29J
Chapel Hill, NC 27516-2826
America Online: lharris
$25
317,479 bytes

Files are the heart of the operating system—and controlling your files means you can control, at least in part, the operating system. FileBuddy gives you that control.

FileBuddy is sort of the Finder's Get Info box on steroids. It displays all of the file's attributes (things like file name, file size, icon, and color). And, unlike the Finder, you can change just about any file attribute.

For instance, if you need to change a file's type or creator (which is something you'll want to do more than once, you can type the new type or creator code into FileBuddy. Can't remember those pesky file codes? Don't sweat it. Show FileBuddy an application or file, and FileBuddy will use the type or creator code for it. You can even change the file's creation or modification date. (If you're like me, you can probably think of hundreds of morally troubling uses for this feature.)

The author, Larry Harris, has been very responsive to my bug reports, and he's added every feature I've requested. (In the interest of fair disclosure, I need to point out that I work with Larry, and I've been beta testing FileBuddy since it first arrived. That probably helps.)

4

Hack Facts

Global Variables
Viewer

APPL
Takashi Suzuki
338-45 Miyagawa Haruno-cho
Shuchi-gun Shizuoka, Japan
Internet:setsu@
lab2.yamaha.co.jp
orGAF03072@
niftyserve.or.jp
$10
51,324 bytes

Your Mac's low-memory region is filled with fascinating global variables. These store all kinds of important values that make your Mac tick. Although Apple always says to ignore these when programming, clearly you can't always do that.

For instance, if you want to hide the menu bar in your program, the way to do it is to save the old menu bar height (which you read from the global variable mBarHeight), change the menu bar height to 0, and then call DrawMenuBar. There's no other way to do it (that I've heard of, at least). But Apple doesn't support tinkering with such low-memory variables, so someday this hack may break.

Notice in Figure 4-5 that GVV displays three important things: the address of the memory location, its length in bytes, and its current value. A description of the value is given also; this is very helpful as there are tons of secret memory locations, and many are poorly documented by Apple.

Does anybody remember the monkey mentioned in Figure 4-5? This was a program that would simulate a user by sending random events to a program. It acts as sort of a virtual user except the monkey could erase files, initialize hard drives, and basically totally wreck your computer much more efficiently than any virtual user. Anyway, thanks to

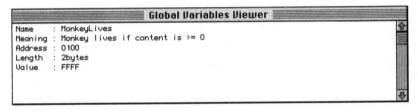

```
Global Variables Viewer
Name     : MonkeyLives
Meaning  : Monkey lives if content is >= 0
Address  : 0100
Length   : 2bytes
Value    : FFFF
```

Figure 4-5.   *You can use the arrow keys to scroll through all the global variables*

GVV, I've had a pleasant reverie, and if I want to bring the monkey back, all I gotta do is put a positive number into memory location $100.

You can search for a global variable by using the program's Find menu item. For example, you could search for *rawmouse* and see the variables' values change as you move the mouse.

You will use thousands of Macintosh ROM routines in the course of writing a Mac program. When programming, it's usually easy to remember which routine to use—for instance, I'll probably never forget that CopyBits draws a bitmap. But it's never easy to remember all the arguments to any particular routine.

Referential Expansion takes care of this by looking up the arguments in the Think Reference database. When you type the name of a routine, and then "(?", Referential Expansion looks up the arguments and types it into your program.

For example, typing this:

```
CopyBits(?
```

gives you these results:

```
CopyBits( &srcMap, &destMap, &srcRect, &destRect,
tMode, maskRgn )
```

If you'd like to read the description of that ROM call, simply exchange the "?" for a ">" symbol:

```
CopyBits(>
```

4

will open that correct page of Think Reference, and move it in front of all other applications.

Other programs exist that do the same kind of thing, but this is my favorite. It's fast and unobtrusive, it doesn't interrupt your work flow, and it makes life so much easier.

Think Reference=Inside Macintosh - Pain - Agony - Paper Cuts

Think Reference is a must-have for any Mac programmer. You can instantly look up all of the ROM calls from Inside Macintosh volumes I through VI. It provides a description, and often some very handy sample code (unfortunately, it's in C). Plus, you can copy the function templates and paste them into your program.

Referential Expansion works in conjunction with Think Reference. You can't use Referential Expansion without it.

Think Reference is the envy of all Windows programmers. Symantec sells it. You should buy it.

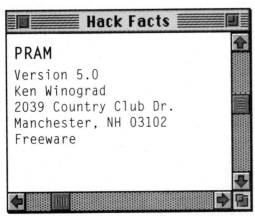

PRAM stands for Parameter RAM, and like those little gnomes who spin the wheels that make your Mac work, every Mac's got some. PRAM is just like regular RAM, except it's backed up by a battery.

When your Mac is turned off or unplugged, this memory stays intact. Things like the current date and time, your background desktop pattern, your serial port settings, and so on are stored there.

PRAM (the freeware program) provides a way to explore the things stored in this special memory. You can see what the speaker volume is, or the number of times the menu blinks, or what the current alarm setting is.

And you can change all of these settings, too. Usually the Finder's control panels offer a much cleaner and easier way of changing these settings, but the Finder's for wimps. Use PRAM.

Note

PRAM can also zap the parameter RAM. Sometimes when a program crashes, it may do hideous things to the parameter RAM and trash all your settings. You'll know this has happened if all of a sudden your settings seem wrong. Zapping the PRAM is the only way back to safety.

Hack Facts

RIPEM Mac
APPL
Raymond Lau
Internet: raylau@mit.edu
Free
156,035 bytes

If anyone wants to send secure, encrypted, digitally-signed files to me, use RIPEM—my public key is included later in this chapter.

If you don't know what I'm talking about, shame on you—you should if you're a frequent e-mail user. Electronic mail can be easily read by any number of people, including your system administrator, America Online staff people, or sneaky snoopers on the Internet, some of whom are quite unsavory. Trust me, if you send four or five e-mail messages a day, someone, somewhere is reading at least part of it. If you doubt this, consider how the Internet works.

Basically, all e-mail on the Internet is just plain text. Although every e-mail has an address and is directed at one or several specific users, anyone with system-level access can read your mail. Generally, this is okay, since you usually trust this person to be honest. But, when you think of the Internet as a cross-connection of many, many computers, you get a sense of just how many people have access to what you write. If you look at the bottom of your Internet e-mail, you can see the path your mail message took, bouncing from machine to machine as it found its way to you. At each step of the way, anyone who wanted to (which includes thousands of misanthropic, bored, and maladjusted comp-sci geeks who manage the local university file server) could have read your mail. It's just text with an address. All they have to do is ignore the address.

You can run what's called a "snooper," and this program will just watch the Internet and return the packets (chunks of data) as they flow past your computer. This can be anything: print jobs, files being transferred, or directory listings. But it's also your e-mail, or (heaven forbid) "private" chat sessions.

but

as the Internet becomes the medium for more and more important and sensitive business documents, you need to consider what you're sending: Is this message something you want your competition to read? Is this correspondence something you want anyone in the general public reading?

The standard analogy is a postcard: all e-mail can be read by anyone who carries it. The only way to keep prying eyes out is with some sort of envelope. Encryption provides an envelope for e-mail.

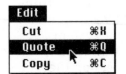

I hold it, that a little rebellion, now and then, is a good thing, and as necessary in the political world as storms in the physical.
—Thomas Jefferson

I don't carry out illegal activities over the Net. I'm not a criminal. But I think my privacy is very important. There are many things that I don't want the entire world to know about (i.e. new book ideas, my awesome secret family lasagna recipe, that I flirt with a friend from college via e-mail). And as I conduct more and more business over the Net, I want all of my business correspondence to be protected.

The simple solution to this problem is encryption. If encryption can be as easy and painless as possible, then it will be used, and the world will be safe for e-mail flirting (or whatever). It's not quite that easy yet. The popular program MacPGP (Pretty Good Privacy), is about as simple to learn and use as a proton accelerator configured in Sanskrit. RIPEM Mac is at least as good, and much easier to figure out.

The slickest feature in both PGP and RIPEM Mac is what's known as public-key cryptography. In both programs, everyone who uses it makes their own secret password.

Traditionally, after you've encrypted something, you have to find a way to tell the recipient what the password is. But if you could communicate via a secure channel in the first place, you wouldn't need to encrypt the message, would you?

RIPEM Mac and PGP use what's known as a public key. When you create your super-secret password, you also create a not-so-secret public key. This, as its name implies, is for the whole world. You can pass this out with impunity.

By some arcane mathematical formula, anything encrypted with your public key can be decrypted only by your private key. So, to send me private mail, you'd encrypt it with my public key, which I send to anyone who asks for it. Then, you send me the encrypted mail, which looks like gibberish. After I get the mail, I decrypt it using my private password. Magic.

PGP vs. RIPEM

there are two big contenders for the Mac encryption throne: PGP and RIPEM. RIPEM, based on the RSA encryption algorithms from RSA Data Security, Inc., was invented in 1977 by Ron Rivest, Adi Shamir, and Leonard Adleman. They have licensed these algorithms to many big computer companies (such as Microsoft, Apple, Sun, and Novell). PGP, on the other hand, was created by Phil Zimmerman, on his own time, from his own algorithms. RSA claims that Zimmerman's work violates their patents; Zimmerman claims that, since he doesn't charge for PGP, it violates nothing.

which is better? Well, PGP is probably stronger encryption. Since Phil Zimmerman was writing his program for himself, he made it as strong as he could. RSA, on the other hand, had to satisfy the demands of the State Department in order to get an export license. Part of what the State Department demands is that the NSA, our National Security Agency, be able to decrypt data in other countries. So it's a safe bet that PGP is more secure than the for-export RSA.

But overall, both are pretty secure. To quote from the RIPEM Mac manual:

"By even generous estimates, an attack against a 512-bit key, the smallest size supported by RIPEM Mac, would take a few years unless mathematical miracles are discovered."

it will be years before anyone breaks these systems, so you're safe for at least that long. (If you're wondering about key size, go with the largest key you can—the larger the key, the more secure the encryption.)

I have chosen RIPEM Mac for my personal use only because the user interface is much, much simpler than PGP's. The encryption used in RIPEM is fast becoming the industry standard. It's even being incorporated in the Internet's upcoming Privacy Enhanced Mail. There are versions for your DOS friends to use. But remember, your mileage may vary.

RIPEM Mac provides some cool features for Mac folks. You can encrypt any file, not just text files, which is truly cool. RIPEM Mac can be controlled via AppleEvents. The author of RIPEM Mac includes QuickKey macros that will automatically encrypt text from the clipboard. Also, RIPEM Mac supports DES triple-encoding, which means even more security.

RSA is the engine behind Apple's System 7 Pro encryption. In theory, you can cross-crypt between System 7 Pro and RIPEM Mac. Encryption is provided automatically in System 7 Pro, and as that gets more and more widespread, I think encryption will be more accepted. In System 7 Pro, it's so amazingly easy to encrypt mail that it doesn't make sense not to.

Here's my public key.

If you'd rather not type it in—which is a real pain—send me e-mail (my address is "RobTerrell@aol.com") and I'll mail it back to you.

```
-----BEGIN PUBLIC KEY-----
User:

Rob Terrell
PublicKeyInfo:

MIGcMAoGBFUIAQECAgQAA4GNADCBiQKBgQDU4PfQ93g6NVUOFxuROVASGL8
9QugZ

/Jh+UvKGD5SZtb2/w2ul2xOLTrSWsYeX24Qb2Lgp1N7Om1yBpfLFshV9zjJ
+BOHT

7XUUFwoQ6kSUdwsoMIkC1m93Bgd96ylcifGH7nC12fL7kPB1ol5aT2Men3i
AWOPy
MLy8G3ae53ukhQIDAQAB
MD5OfPublicKey: 40CC406B74716C5DAA72CE77E7219728
-----END PUBLIC KEY-----
```

Anyone who wants to send mail that they don't want an unintentional audience reading should use RIPEM or PGP, or an equivalent program. I don't care which you use (unless you want to send secure mail to me!), just pick one horse and stick with it.

Hack Facts

ROMmie
APPL
Version 1.0
Rolan Misson
roland.mansson@ldc.lu.se
Public domain
32,648 bytes

ROMmie is a tiny application that scans your Mac's ROM, makes a list of everything it finds, and dumps the entire contents to your disk.

While it's not legal to do anything with this ROM dump (after all, it's still the property of Apple Computer) it's fun to look through and see what you can find.

ROMmie outputs a ResEdit file, so you can browse through and look at the different resources. Check the SND resource, which contains interesting sounds. Why are they there? Only Apple engineers know.

Also, there have been some hidden pictures of Apple engineers stuck in the ROMs of various Macs over the years. ROMmie is a great way to find and display these pictures.

PICT pirates and CDEV commander—

sacking through Apps with ResEdit: ResEdit is the only must-have tool I can recommend. Every certified Macgeek needs to keep this one handy.

ResEdit, as its name implies, allows you to edit res. Ha ha. I mean, ResEdit allows you to edit resources. What's a resource? If you don't know, then you're definitely on the left side of the bell curve for readers of this book, but I'll explain anyway.

All Mac files—that is, everything on your hard drive—can contain two kinds of stuff. In the data fork of a file, data gets stored (i.e. as I type this book and save it, the words go into the data fork of the file). But there's a schizophrenic split, and some files also have resource forks. In the resource fork you can store icons, pictures, sounds, code, just about anything. Applications are generally all resources. Very little exists in the data fork of most applications. For a better explanation of what resources are, check volume I of Inside Macintosh.

ResEdit lets you snoop inside programs. See that cool picture in the About box of Photoshop? Want to lift it for your startup screen? No problemo, chief. Copy and Paste in ResEdit and you're done.

ResEdit often is the easiest, most efficient way to personalize and modify your Mac and the programs you run on that faithful machine of yours. Plus, ResEdit hacks are usually extremely visible and can affect some fundamental "look and feel" aspects of programs, making it seem as though you did a lot more work than you actually did, which in turn can make you seem far brighter, which in turn can help to win over potential mates.

All of that is true up until that last part, sadly. But you really can use ResEdit for quick, fun hacks. In the System file itself, for example, some simple and fun icon-related hacks can be quite safely made. (Keep in mind this is your System file I'm talking about, so don't go nuts.) For example, let's say you had a special symbol or your initials, or something like that that you would just love to have on all of your folders. Sure, you could just use System 7's Get Info copy-and-paste method to change icon types after you've toyed with the icon in some image-manipulation program, but then you would have to cut and paste every time you created a new folder. What a hassle.

Open up ResEdit instead. Then open your System file, OK your way through the warnings, and find the icon marked ICL8. Double-click on that. You should see a big screen full of all of the icons the System normally uses. Just pick the one you want to modify, in this case the folder, and click twice on it. You'll see more warnings. Just, you know, accept them. Now look! A nifty icon-editing window! Change the icon as you wish, close the window, and boom! Custom icons, always ready. The floppy icon is also good to change, and it's always fun to put yucky stuff dripping out of the trash as well. Maybe add some flies, too.

One note

My friend modified the Centris 610 icon so it would be his custom one in the "About This Macintosh" window. It never worked. The icon appeared all weird. Nothing else, though.

ResEdit is also useful for modifying other software. Take the popular shareware screen saver, DarkSide. DarkSide has a module called "Snowblower" which has this nice animation of snow blowing out of this blocky and boring looking Binford snowblower. With ResEdit, a friend who digs VWs found the PICT files for that module, and pasted a picture of his bug over the boring snowblower. Now, when his screen saver kicks in, there's a nice personal image of his yellow bug with some weasel leaning out the window spraying everywhere.

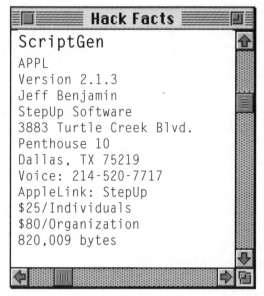

Hack Facts

```
ScriptGen
APPL
Version 2.1.3
Jeff Benjamin
StepUp Software
3883 Turtle Creek Blvd.
Penthouse 10
Dallas, TX 75219
Voice: 214-520-7717
AppleLink: StepUp
$25/Individuals
$80/Organization
820,009 bytes
```

At some point, every Mac developer will need to make an installer. The Apple Installer—that thing you ran when you first got your computer, or whenever you get new software from Apple—provides a simple, friendly interface and a painless user experience. Most Mac users have no problem using the Apple Installer.

Contrast this with programmers, who have great problems working with the Apple Installer. The internal workings of the Installer are pure hell incarnate—a weird stew of odd resource types that must be created with exactly the right IDs. It's very difficult to make one right.

ScriptGen provides a simple, intuitive, point-and-click way to create those Installer resources. In short, you load up the floppies, decide where everything will be saved on the user's hard drive, and save the script. ScriptGen creates the necessary Installer file, and you're ready to go!

Of course nothing is that simple. There're tons of options: you can create a splash screen for your installer (and ScriptGen even provides painting tools to do this, as Figure 4-6 shows).

There's no better way to create installer scripts than ScriptGen. And using Apple's installer is a good idea for your beleaguered users, who have to figure out how to use all this stuff.

ScriptGen vs. ScriptGen Pro

Whereas ScriptGen is a shareware product, ScriptGen Pro is a commercial product written by the same author. Many users believe it provides an even easier interface with more control over the installer scripts it generates.

Also, Aladdin Software offers InstallerMaker, which is based on its StuffIt technology. InstallerMaker is no harder to

Figure 4-6. *ScriptGen gives you painting tools to create your installer's splash screen*

master than StuffIt Deluxe, but it creates very powerful installer programs. Plus, it will compress all of the files you're installing, so it saves on floppy disks.

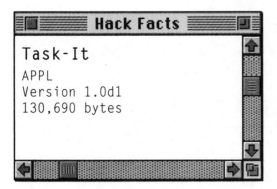

When System 7 came out, it included the Process Manager. This example of toolbox wizardry gave Mac users something UNIX programmers enjoyed for years: the ability to ask the system about the programs that were running—called processes, or *tasks*—and find out how much RAM they were using, or how much processor time they were bogging down.

Note

UNIX is the operating system used most by universities, researchers, and government sites. Most high-end workstations (Silicon Graphics, Sun Microsystems, and so forth) come with UNIX. You can get UNIX for your Macintosh, but I don't recommend it since there's no real advantage to using it on the Mac.

BYTE's Mac Programmer's Cookbook

Task-It gives a glimpse inside the Process Manager. It shows a window that lists all of the current processes. And, as shown in Figure 4-7, Task-It can tell you which program is taking all the processor's time.

Note in Figure 4-7 the listings for "File Sharing Extension" and "Express Modem." The small "ß" character in front of these indicates that the process is running in the background, and hence there's no way to call it to the front or interact with it. Sometimes you'll want to quit these background processes. But how can you, since there's no way to interact with them?

Task-It can stop a process at any time. By selecting a process and then performing Kill Process (under the "Action" pop-up menu), the process will be sent to the great RAM disk in the sky.

Also note that this is a way to turn off file sharing—just kill the "File Sharing Extension" process. It may not be as easy as using the Sharing Setup control panel, but it'll impress your friends that much more, especially if you toss around some serious techno-jargon while you're doing it. ("I would use the control panel, but all the diatronic waves are reversing the polarity.") Then again, they'll probably just think you're a geek.

Task	Type	Crt	Time	Hog	Free	Heap
Finder	FNDR	MACS	2:44	0%	23K	324K
ß File Sharing Extension	INIT	hhgg	0:05	0%	23K	167K
ß Express Modem	cdev	3615	0:20	8%	52K	433K
DarkSide	APPL	DSOM	0:14	7%	267K	300K
Microsoft Word	APPL	MSWD	1:47	1%	766K	2048K
BaseToBase	dfil	movr	1:32	40%	7K	19K

Task-It   Action ▼   Total Memory: 32768K
                       ~Free Memory: 24155K

Figure 4-7. *Task-It's window lets you see which program is hogging the processor time*

Hack Facts

Hell's Programmer Font
FFIL (Font)
Version 1.1
Paul Cunningham
P.O. Box 1923
Mango, FL 33550-1923
CompuServe: 75020,3540
Internet: 75020.3540@
compuserve.com

Since time immemorial (which means 1984 on the Macintosh), programmers as a rule have been using the Monaco font to display their code. Why use such a boring, mundane font? Well, the answer is steeped in history. The Mac was the first computer to use proportionally spaced fonts in its display. (Well, not the first, but the first one that anyone bought.)

At the time of the Mac's introduction, I heard many people ask, "But can it display 80 columns of text?" Apple's official answer was "yes, using the Monaco font," although it should have been "yes, but why in God's name would you want to?" The 80-column display was a barbaric convention forced upon us by the limitations of early computers. Proportionally spaced type, which is the way type appears in newspapers, magazines, and this book among others, feels much more natural.

Programmers know the usefulness of monospaced type. If you are writing a program, it helps to line up sections of code at the same horizontal tab mark. And most programming editors don't deal with proportional fonts very well.

The problem with Monaco is that it's remained unchanged since 1984, and it contains the same oversights it had back then. For instance, the number *1* and the letter *l* are indistinguishable from one another. The zero and the capital *O* are also identical. And there's no support for the nonstandard Mac menu bar characters.

Hell's Programmer Font solves these problems nicely. It starts with the basic Monaco font, with the characters spaced a little bit tighter, so you can see more lines of code in a window. It then adds distinguishing marks to similar-looking characters, such as a slash to the zero. And it also adds control characters, so you can see when you've typed a CONTROL-L (which is a line feed) into a text string.

No matter what language you program in, you will find this font useful.

Hack Facts

WindowShade

CDEV
Version 1.2
Rob Johnston
26,192 bytes

On Macs with small screens—PowerBooks especially—windows tend to proliferate. And it always seems that the window you want is piled under tons of other windows.

WindowShade can help. This control panel watches your mouse clicks and, when you double-click in a window's title bar, it shrinks the window down to just the title bar.

You can still drag this title bar around. It's still a window in the respect that you can reorder it with other windows, or close it, or zoom it. But until you double-click in the title bar, its contents are hidden.

You can choose to have a sound play—an appropriate "shoop"—when the window is shrunken or expanded. I've found that this level of tactile feedback really helps new users understand what has just happened.

For programmers especially—for whom there are endless windows filled with source code files—WindowShade is a godsend.

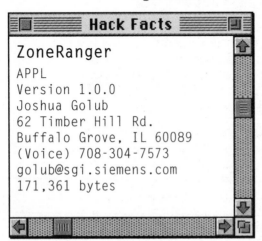

Hack Facts

ZoneRanger

APPL
Version 1.0.0
Joshua Golub
62 Timber Hill Rd.
Buffalo Grove, IL 60089
(Voice) 708-304-7573
golub@sgi.siemens.com
171,361 bytes

Inside the Macintosh, every application runs in its own "heap zone." If you wanted to look at the heap, traditionally you'd explore it with a debugger such as Macsbug. But thanks to ZoneRanger, you can do it just by pointing and clicking.

ZoneRanger lists all of the currently running programs in its Overview window, as shown in Figure 4-8. You can see a graphical representation of the amount of memory a program is using (as in "About the Finder" from the Finder's Apple menu). You also can see the number of different types of memory blocks. For instance, in Figure 4-8, the Finder has allocated only 12 pointers. That's pretty good (competent programmers use handles instead of pointers, since handles are relocatable blocks).

Pointers vs. handles

Pointer = indicates the starting address of a block of memory. This memory can't be moved by the system, or else when you tried to use the pointer, it would be invalid.

Handle = indicates a pointer to an area of memory. This memory can be moved, since using the handle instead of the pointer allows the pointer to be changed willy-nilly by the system.

Confused? Read Inside Macintosh: Memory *(Addison Wesley, New York, 1992).*

4

**   File   Edit   Configure   Special**

Overview

Name	Free Blocks	Pointers	Handles...	🔒	✏️	🗄️
System	229	569	2778	271	241	279
MultiFinder	6	2	107	36	13	0
Finder	21	12	116	14	46	65
Express Modem	7	25	23	17	11	12
DarkSide	18	5	51	1	3	7
Microsoft Word	18					70
File Buddy 2.0...	52					56
TeachText	29					13
ZoneRanger 1.0...	12					15

Zone: DarkSide
Count: 5
Size: 1264

Type	Size	Attr	Type	ID	Name
Pointer	272	●	...	......	......
Pointer	272	●	...	......	......
Pointer	272	●	...	......	......
Pointer	272	●	...	......	......
Pointer	176	●	...	......	......

Options...

Figure 4-8. *ZoneRanger shows the various types of blocks of memory in an interactive, easy-to-browse fashion*

ZoneRanger can do three things to a heap zone:

- Compact it, which moves relocatable blocks so that a large chunk of contiguous memory is available.

- Purge it, which deletes all purgeable and unlocked handles.

- Compact and Purge, to see the maximum amount of memory available in your program's heap.

ZoneRanger also lets you open a graphical view of any heap zone. Pointers and handles are shown in different colors. Locked, purgeable, and resource bits of handles are shown via special highlight colors. By clicking on any block, you can see the block's address and other flag bits. Also, clicking on a block shows some of the data stored in that block. You can dump that data to a disk file or the clipboard for further study. As shown in Figure 4-9, ZoneRanger shows a memory map of the program in question. When you click on a block of memory, it shows the actual data held by each block; you

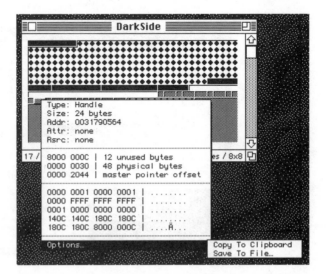

Figure 4-9. *ZoneRanger shows a memory map of the program DarkSide*

can dump the listing to the clipboard or a file for further examination. Notice all the diamonds on the top of the screen in Figure 4-9: these indicate that the block is from a resource file.

the one fault I have with ZoneRanger is that the amount of free space is not immediately obvious. Knowing how much space you have would be helpful for those times when you're trying to track down memory leaks.

Coming Up Next—Getting External

In Chapter 5, we'll be surveying a wide range of external commands for use with HyperCard, AppleScript, and other programming environments. If you've ever spent hours trying to custom-craft a special piece of code to take care of a problem that you're sure everyone else has encountered as well, then the odds are someone else has already solved the problem. Check out the external commands in the next chapter if you still doubt me.

4

011010 11000110 0011010 11001001 100010001

11010 11000110 0011010 11001001 100010001

0011010 11001001 100010001

part 2

The Hard Stuff

External Commands: Help for the Working Stiff

A friend of mine is a big fan of Volkswagen Beetles. His little yellow bug is less a method of locomotion than it is a hobby. His somewhat blind love for those odd little cars causes him, knowingly or not, to analogize nearly anything born, forged, or smelt into the terms of the VW Bug.

Usually when he does this I dismiss it with a roll of my eyes and that finger-gagging motion or sometimes I twirl my index finger next to my ear in the international gesture for insanity. But recently, he had an analogy that actually came close to being useful—one that was astute enough for me not to attribute it to the sad rantings of a machine-obsessed madman. It dealt with things called external commands.

External commands, or XCMDs, are electronic beasts that work with high-level languages, such as HyperTalk, to help them (and you) use these scripting tongues to do things their original builders never thought you could do. These external commands (ranted my friend) are a lot like third-party and aftermarket accessories to his beloved Volkswagen.

Load the code

Externals are code resources—technically, they are resources of type code. To use them in a HyperCard stack, open both the stack and the external command file in ResEdit. Simply copy the code resource from the external command file into the stack you need it in. The name of the code resource is the actual command you type in HyperCard to make it work.

For example, the external "Flash", which flashes the Mac's screen, is a code resource named (oddly enough) "Flash". The resource ID doesn't matter; just make sure it doesn't conflict with any other code resources.

You can add code resources to a HyperCard stack until you run out of disk space or the resource manager can't handle any more stuff, which in my experience is around 15 MB.

When the Volkswagen was first built out of the ruins of a war-torn factory in Wolfsburg, no one thought it would be popular. Were they ever wrong! Just remember, there's never been a series of Disney movies about a sentient Corvair. Anyway, as much as people loved the bug, and as tough and fine a car as it was, it had limitations that the factory had no pressing urge to address. So others did.

Want to make your little four-cylinder bug go faster? Easy. Look through one of the many aftermarket catalogs and pick up a dual-carb system, some headers, a mechanical-advance distributor, or maybe some bigger bolt-on cylinders. Want to make it last longer? Order an external oil cooler. Go through deep mud? A limited-slip transaxle. Too cold? A gas heater. Not funky enough? Headlight visors. And so on.

Quote

A watch that's fast, that's ahead, at least it keeps time. But a watch that's behind doesn't keep time, you know that.
—Bill Hughes

All of these add-ons are the Volkswagen equivalent of XCMDs. The original doesn't quite do what you need, the company doesn't really care, and you can't fake it, so build it and bolt it on. Just make sure it hooks up in all the right places, and you're set. Whether it's a color TIFF in HyperCard or a 6-to-12 volt converter for your old '61, it's the same principle. One's better for desktop publishing, but the other one's louder.

I hear some guy in Seattle converts bugs to electrical power, so maybe someday high-level scripting languages and VWs will converge. Maybe.

Volksware: HyperCard, 4D, and So Forth

Let's say you're just getting into programming the Mac. Let's say you have little or no programming experience. And let's say you have a life and can't spend the rest of the summer learning how to do this stuff.

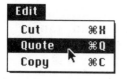

We go about our daily lives understanding almost nothing of the world.

—Carl Sagan

What you need is a tool—something that does 90 percent of the programming for you. Like the fabled Volkswagen, you need something you can add attachments to until you've got the super-coup of your dreams.

You can do so much with an environment like HyperCard, but sometimes there are things you just can't do. There are certain things, usually dealing directly with the Macintosh Toolbox ROMs, that you'll need external commands to handle. Don't sweat it. That's why we're at Chapter 5.

Believe it or not, you can create some amazing programs using these tools. The company I work for has shipped several commercial products based on both HyperCard and 4D. Not every problem can be solved in HyperCard or 4D; sometimes you've just got to bite the bullet and do it in C or Pascal (or hire some code warrior to do it for you).

But sometimes you can straddle the line, write most of your cool program in something quick, easy, and painless like HyperCard, and do the rest through external commands. Plus, you can get external commands for more than just

HyperCard. Just about every scripting-language-based tool supports external commands, including:

- **AppleScript** Apple's system-wide scripting language loads external commands from "Scripting Addition" files (which technically are known as *OSAXes* or by the more hip but silly plural *OSAXen*).

- **4th Dimension** This popular database program supports 4DEXes (which is just the company's name for an external command). Sadly, there is not a large collection of high-quality 4DEXes out there in netland.

- **Foxbase Pro** Microsoft's entry in the database wars can use XCMDs created for the older versions of HyperCard (that is, XCMDs that don't try to create special external windows).

Since HyperCard has been wildly popular, there are tons more XCMDs for it than there are 4DEXes for 4th Dimension. Since AppleScript is fairly new, there's not yet a wide range of external commands to choose from. However, with these external commands, you can still do powerful new things in any of the environments, such as:

- open new windows to display text or pictures

- scan the hard drive for files, or get the contents of folders

- connect to servers over AppleShare or even TCP/IP

And so on. The whole point of external commands is to give you the power to improve the system. The designers couldn't anticipate everything, so they gave a reasonable amount of functionality. If you need more, hey, go build it yourself and tack it on. It's totally modular.

Building your own XCMD with tools you have around the home

Creating external commands is addictive. It's not a terribly difficult programming task, since by definition most externals are short, sweet, one-hit wonders. Although it's a little bit different for every environment, a few basic principles remain the same.

In a nutshell, an external command is just a code resource; there's no header, the first thing in the resource is the first instruction. (Compare this to the business of writing desk accessories or drivers, which can use complicated headers.)

Your externals can receive parameters. In OSAXen, you must unwrap your parameters from their Apple Event Containers. In HyperCard, up to 16 parameters are given to your XCMD in a big array.

All Mac compilers will generate a single code resource from your program. If your external command gets really big, you can find yourself over the 32K limit for code resources. The Think compilers have an option to generate code resources that break the 32K limit. It's quite painless to use, and as a bonus, you get to use global variables (which code resources normally can't access).

The actual hows and whys can get pretty complicated, and really is the subject of another book. In fact, Gary Bond's XCMDs for HyperCard (MIS Press: Portland, Oregon, 1988), although out of date, is a great source to learn more about how and why.

Also, check online or with your favorite neighborhood SmartFriend.

Mac-Crazed University + Cheap Student Labor = Externals with Zing!

Dartmouth was one of the first schools that Apple seeded with Macintoshes, and has been a hotbed of Mac fanaticism ever since. Dartmouth's computer whizzes have produced some incredible teaching tools and more than their share of shareware, as well as multimedia student orientation guides long before "multimedia" became a corporate buzzword.

HyperCard also has been the object of fanatical reverence at Dartmouth. Its strengths and weaknesses were discovered long ago, and over time a whole series of XCMDs were developed to overcome these limitations. (See Figure 5-1.)

Many of the XCMDs show their age. For instance, the commands that let you create your own menus in the menu bar are definitely outdated—HyperCard's had that capability since version 2.0 came out many years ago.

All of the authors are affiliated with Dartmouth. You can use these XCMDs freely in your own stacks, but any commercial distribution requires an agreement with Dartmouth.

Quote

This was for me the greatest contradiction in my life; getting money for showing up at campus to tell students to burn down their schools.

—Jerry Rubin

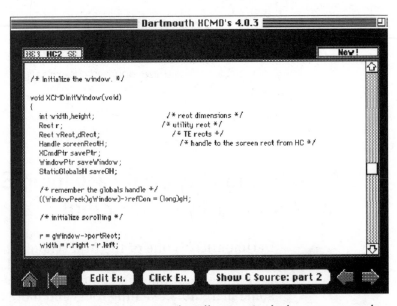

Figure 5-1. *The Dartmouth collection includes source code for most of the XCMDs*

The authors of the XCMDs are all HyperCard experts. Some XCMDs were created by Kevin Calhoun, who later became Apple's lead engineer on the HyperCard 2.1 project.

The following is the full list of XCMDs with short descriptions of each:

XCMD	DESCRIPTION
AuxActive	Returns TRUE if A/UX (Apple's UNIX) is currently running.
BinaryFile	Reads and writes binary (i.e. non-text) files. Useful if you want to read another program's data files.
ChooserName	Returns the user's name as it is stored in the Chooser (System 6) or the Sharing Setup control panel (System 7).
Clipboard	Lets you get or set the clipboard contents (text only; sorry, no pictures).
ClipToPICT	Creates a PICT resource from the image on the clipboard, and adds it to the current stack's resource fork.
CompareStrings	Performs a case-sensitive comparison of two strings, and returns the range of characters that do not match.
ConvertDate	Works like HyperCard's standard date conversion routines, but works for a larger range of dates. Instead of January 1, 1904 to February 6, 2040, ConvertDate works from January 1, 0001 to December 31, 9999.
DeleteRes	Deletes a resource from the current stack.
DeleteResFork	Deletes the resource fork of a stack while leaving the data fork untouched; good for a total cleansing of all icons, pictures, and other junk that accumulates there.
DelimitedChunk	Gets an item in a text string, given the character used to delimit the items. Not so useful since you can now (since version 2.0) set HyperCard's item delimiter yourself.
EditWindow	Opens an editable text window.

5

XCMD	DESCRIPTION
FileToClip	Copies a text file to the clipboard.
FileToField	Copies a text file to a given field.
FileToPICTRes	Copies a picture from a PICT or PTNG file, and adds the resource to the current stack.
FindInField	Finds the given string in a field. Returns the character offset where the string begins.
FindKey	Searches the given field for a character string. Unlike FindInField, you can specify the character position to start from.
GetFieldText, DisposeFieldText, SetFieldText	These three commands let you copy styled text between fields.
GetResources	Copies all XCMD, XFCN, and other specified resources from a source file into the current stack.
HC Utilities	These are a set of low-level C functions that XCMD authors might find useful.
HyperFolder	Returns the path to the currently running copy of HyperCard. Useful? Probably not.
IsResource	Returns TRUE if the specified resource exists in the current stack.
LastVisibleChar	Returns the position of the last character that can be seen in a text field.
LeafName	Removes the path from a filename.
ListDialog	Displays a dialog with a list box. You can specify several optional buttons as well. Returns the selection of the list, and the name of the button that was pressed.
ListWindow	Opens a window containing a list of objects.
MenuHandler	Adds a menu to HyperCard's menu bar.
ModalDialog	Displays any dialog box stored in a DLOG resources in the current stack.
MultiSort	Sorts the contents of a field by any item of each line. Works numerically and alphabetically, in both descending and ascending order.
ObjectExists	Returns TRUE if the specified object actually exists.

XCMD	DESCRIPTION
Password	Hides the password as you type it, unlike HyperCard's Password command.
PICTFileToRes	Creates a PICT resource from a PICT file.
PictureShow, PictureHide	Displays a picture in a window, and hides the window.
PopList	Creates a popup menu that displays the text you specify.
PrintField	Prints the contents of a field.
PrintPictRes	Prints a picture from the resource fork.
RandOrder	Reorders a container randomly by word, line, or character.
Replace	Searches through the text in a container for a specified string, and optionally replaces it with another string.
ReplaceChar	Replaces all occurrences of one character with another.
ResList	Lists the resources in a file.
Rinstall	Copies any resource to any specified file.
SerialHandler	Opens, reads from, writes to, and closes the serial ports.
SizeCardWindow	Makes the card window a different size. Totally redundant since HyperCard version 2.0.
SortField	Sorts a field alphabetically.
SortFieldByItem	Sorts a field based on an item of each line.
SystemFolder	Returns the path to the currently active system folder.
TDWindow	Displays styled text in a window.
TextStream	Dumps text items directly to your laser printer for output; is much faster than other printing methods, but uses the printer's default font (usually Courier).
WritePermission	Returns TRUE if the specified file can be written to.
WriteToFile	Dumps a container to a text file.

5

Although many of the Dartmouth XCMDs righted wrongs that were rectified in later versions of HyperCard, there are still some gems and jewels among them. I'm especially fond of these XCMDs:

- **Clipboard** because I often want to dump some variable to the clipboard.

- **SerialHandler** because it's small and an easy-to-use way to send serial data from HyperCard.

Check them out yourself, and see which you add to your collection. If you use any of them in a commercial stack, don't forget to contact Dartmouth regarding licensing issues.

One of the oldest collections of externals for HyperCard has to be Developer Stack. Developer Stack boasts a simple interface. You can scroll the collection of externals and, if you like, try them out as you go. You don't have to guess about whether an external will suit your purpose!

I like this collection's breadth. It offers a little bit of everything, but it doesn't push the size envelope. One of my favorites in here is OSErr. Simply pass OSErr an error code (from any other XCMD or from HyperCard) and it will display a dialog box that explains the error in sane English instead of computerese.

Over time, many people have contributed to Developer Stack. It's a well-known resource for XCMD writers and users. If you've written an XCMD that you think the world should know about, send it to Steve at one of the addresses given in the Hack Fact.

One problem: under HyperCard 2.2, the index buttons don't work (look at the seven buttons along the bottom of the window shown in Figure 5-2). For some reason, the DialogList external displays give you one very long line

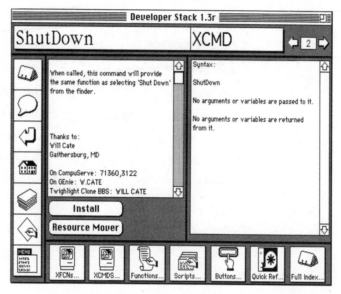

Figure 5-2. *As you browse the Developer Stack, you can use the "install" button to copy the commands you like into your own stacks*

5

containing all of the items, instead of a list of items that you can select from. Bummer, dude. Let's hope Steve gets on this soon.

AboutMe	CheckMenu
Alert	CheckString
ArrowKeys	ClipToPICTRes
ART HyperText Trick	Color
AutoScroll	CombineFile
BarButton	Commands
ChangeCase	CommInit
ChangeFileType	CommRead
ChangeMenu	CommWrite
ChangeObjectLayer	CompactStacks

Constants

Control Structures

convertDate

CopyFile

CStoHCdateconversion

daysBetweenDates

DeleteFile

DeleteFile2

DeleteMenu

DeProtect

DispPict

Dogear

DoList

doRestart

DragOn

DrawPict

Ejector

EnableMenu

FileAtRoot

FileCreator

FileExists

FileLength

FileModDate

FileName

Files

FileType

FileVisFlag

FontName

FontSizesize

FormatNum

FormatNumPadded

FormatPhoneNum

Functions

GetDANames

GetFullPath

GetVolume

HPopUpMenu

HyperSND

Import

ImportPict

initialCaps

InitMidi

InKey

InsertInList

Interpolate

isRunning

LastOffset

LastPathComponent

LastPathItem

LineNumber

lower

massCompact

MenuBar

MergeStacks

More Dog Ears

MoveFile

MultiFinder

MungeMCTB

NewFileName	sendSerial
NewMenu	SetFile
noButtonDelete	SetVolume
noFieldDelete	ShowMenu
NumberofChars	ShowScripts
NumberOfDAs	ShutDown
OSErr	Slider
PathItems	sortItems
PinPointer	SortReals
PopUp	SortRealsII
PopUpMenu	SoundCapToRes
PowerCreate	Speak
PowerToggle	StdFile
PrintClip	Strip
Progress	StripNum
Properties	Stripper
ReadCat	subLaunch
RenameFile	SumInt
ResCopy	System Messages
ResetMIDI	Tabs2Spaces
ResetPrinter	Talk
Resources	Text Import
ReturnkeyInField	thePixel
rnd	TitleBar
RxMIDI	TxMIDI
ScreenSize	upper
Scroll Text Button 1	VolumeName
ScrollingFields	ZipCheck
Self Naming Button	

5

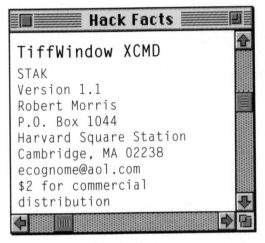

TIFF is a picture file format that is supposedly platform-independent, resolution-independent, and colorspace-model-independent. In practice it's actually pretty darn dependent, but still it's one of the most popular bitmapped graphics file formats.

Trust me, you don't want to write TIFF file reading code; it's a huge chore. I did it—once. I'll never do it again—mainly because I can reuse my code. But you can't reuse my code, or I'll sue you till your ears bleed, so you need a tool like TIFFWindow.

And this tool is a breeze to use. This XCMD opens a window to display a TIFF file. You just specify the file to be opened and a bunch of parameters for the window: size, location, zoom level, and so on.

TIFF = Tagged Image File Format

The window it opens is a standard HyperCard XWindow, which means it handles all of the usual window events (redraw, activate, deactivate, and so on) with the usual aplomb. Figure 5-3 shows a picture that I drew in MacPaint (well, sort of) displayed in a window created by TIFFWindow.

I've never run into any bombs or bugs while using this external command. It's solid enough for my uses, and probably even for a commercial release. So if you're making a commercial application with HyperCard and you need to display TIFFs, then you could do much worse than TIFFWindow.

And, as a bonus, TIFFWindow comes with its C source code. If you need to modify the source code to handle another nonstandard part of the TIFF "standard" (for instance, 16-bit color TIFFs), then just add the requisite code and recompile. Or, take the code apart to learn how to make your own TIFF reader program.

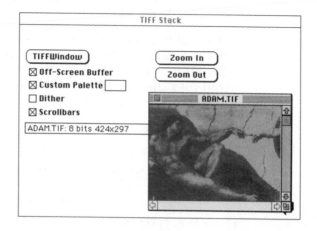

Figure 5-3. *Elitist art reappropriated for the people thanks to TIFFWindow*

Quote

You can't be perfect holding things in your hand all the time, you've got to drop something once in a while.

—Gene Edwards

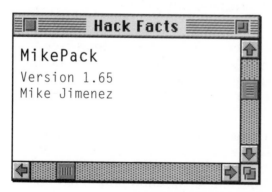

There aren't many complete packages of 4D externals out there despite 4D's immense popularity with the Mac database community. This doesn't surprise me too much because the size of the Mac database community pales in comparison to the Mac HyperCard community.

You'll find many one-shot 4D externals posted on the info-macarchive: externals that work with Microsoft Mail, externals that control list areas, externals that deal with pictures, and so on. But MikePack is the only complete package of externals I could find—and it's a doozy. The more than 30 externals in this package can do things that 4D just can't handle or that 4D normally does very slowly.

Not being much of a 4D whiz, I pawned the actual task of looking at these externals to my friend, Glenn Clingroth. (The latest version of 4D that I have, 2.2.3, doesn't load the demo files that come with this package.) Glenn recommends this package for any serious 4D programmer.

My favorites (well, actually Glenn's favorites) include these four:

- **MP Array2Clip** Copies an array variable to the clipboard. This and MP Pict2Clip are essential if you plan to make a stand-alone application.

- **MP Pict2Clip** Copies a 4D picture variable to the clipboard.

- **MP MergeArrays** Combines any two arrays you send it.

- **MP MoveWindow** Moves any window to a specified location on the screen. This is very handy for getting those dang 4D windows exactly where you want them.

MikePack comes with a handy-dandy installer program, shown in Figure 5-4. You can use this to install just the set of externals you're interested in. This is especially handy for those 4D users who aren't real ResEdit jockeys.

mike's externals may be brilliant, but his readmes aren't all that smart. He gives complete documentation, very good examples, and no e-mail address, no phone number—not even an address that the U.S. Postal Service could use.

So how does one register these extensions? I have no clue. How much money does Mike ask for them? He doesn't say in the documentation or in the readme. Mike, my man, drop me a line at RobTerrell@aol.com and let me know how to pay you!

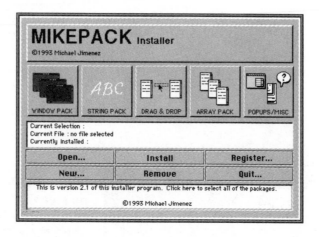

Figure 5-4. *The easy-to-use installer program provides context-sensitive help.*

5

MP APPLY2ARRAY	MP FRAMERECT
MP Array2Clip	MP Gestalt
MP Array2File	MP JustifyText
MP Array2Text	MP MERGEARRAYS
MP ARRAYSELECT	MP MOVEWINDOW
MP DISTINCT	MP MultiDrag
MP DragBlock	MP N2S_Array
MP DragItem	MP PadText
MP DragText	MP Pict2Clip
MP DRAWTEXT	MP POPULATE
MP ERASERECT	MP PopupMenu
MP FILE2TEXT	MP PopupPlus
MP FILLARRAY	MP S2N_Array

MP SCROLLRECT   MP TrimLeft

MP SCROLLTEXT   MP TrimRight

MP SearchArray   MP TrimText

MP SIZEWINDOW   MP WINDOWLOC

MP TEXT2ARRAY   MP WINDOWSIZE

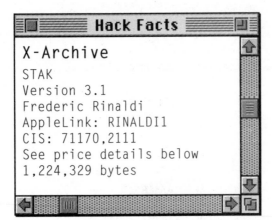

Hack Facts

X-Archive
STAK
Version 3.1
Frederic Rinaldi
AppleLink: RINALDI1
CIS: 71170,2111
See price details below
1,224,329 bytes

Sure, lots of annoying geeks make icons of their faces. And many even plaster their works with these same self-serving icons. But this geek has more than enough programming prowess to back it up. Ladies and gentlemen, I give you...Frederic Rinaldi and his amazing XCMDs!

This is the definitive collection of external commands and functions for HyperCard. If you get no other collection, get this one. This has all the good stuff. The documentation stack is elegantly designed, as Figure 5-5 shows, and lets you try out commands as you learn about them. Frederic's XCMDs are widely used by the HyperCard developer community. The collection is free for unlimited non-commercial use with mention of the author's name and copyright, but commercial use must be licensed and acknowledged by the author.

Rinaldi (and his external commands) have a fantastic reputation in the HyperCard universe because Rinaldi's XCMDs are well-designed, tested, and debugged. The stack describes each in full detail. It even lists all of the error messages you may encounter while using the command.

Thanks for Caring:

One convention of XCMDs and XFCNs is that, whenever "?" is passed as a parameter, the XCMD should put the author's name into HyperCard's message box; when "!" is passed in, the XCMD should display version information.

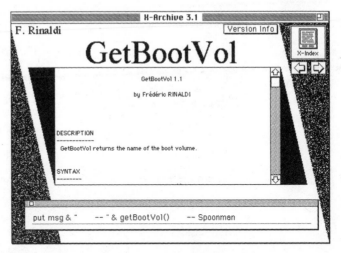

Figure 5-5. *The elegant design of Frederie Rinaldi's documentation stack*

To paraphrase some guy, Christopher Marlowe I think, this rule is honored more in the breach than the observance. Our mortal enemy, the Lazy Programmer, usually doesn't bother adding the few lines of code it takes to supply this information.

Frederic Rinaldi ain't lazy. All of his XCMDs provide this information. It's as much for his benefit (so you know who to thank) as it is for your benefit (so you see if you're using the latest version or not). I wish more folks were like Frederic.

Bet Ya Can't Pick Just One

What follows is a list of every XCMD in Frederic's collection. I am not going to explain every last one, as the names are fairly self-explanatory. Plus, the documentation is a killer, and since I'm insisting that you download it anyway, you'll get more info then. Right?

Align 2.7	Calendoid 1.4
ArchiveContent 1.0	CapsLock 1.0
ATalkZones 1.5	ChooseColor 1.1

Chooser 1.7

ClipInfo 1.0

ClipToPict 1.4

CompressPictFile 1.2

CopyFolder 2.1

CopyRes 2.0

CreateAlias 1.0

CreateCustomIcon 1.1

CreateFolder 1.2

CreateMenuHelp 1.0

CreateMenuHelp -2

CreateStack 1.1

CreateThumbnail 1.2

DateConverter 1.2

DateSort 1.0

DocCreator 1.5

DocTypes 1.6

DoMenu 1.0

EraseFile 1.2

ExtractItems 1.4

FileCopy 2.6

FileIsOpen 1.2

FileMaker 1.2

FileSharingMaster 1.0

FindFolder 1.1

FolderSize 1.4

FontMaster 1.3

FormatNum 1.0

FullBalloons 1.0

FullDrag 1.3

FullFind 1.4

FullHPop 1.5

FullMove 1.2

FullOffset 1.0

FullRemove 1.1

FullRename 1.4

FullReplace 1.1

FullResList 2.1

FullSFPack 1.7

FullSFPut 1.3

FullSort 3.5

FullSort -2

FullSort -3

FullText 1.0

GetBootVol 1.1

GetDir 2.2

GetFInfo 1.3

GetIcon 1.0

GetMode 1.3

GetPassword 1.3

GetSysFolder 1.0

GetVInfo 1.0

GlobalList 1.1	PPCList 1.0
GlobalMaster 1.0	PrinterInfo 1.0
HowMany 1.1	PrintPICT 1.4
ICNToICON 1.8	PrintPictList 1.2
Infoid 1.1	Privileges 1.3
IsDate 1.0	Prompt 2.5
IsFile 1.0	Promptoid 1.5
IsFinderLocked 1.2	QCopy 1.2
IsFolder 1.0	RemoveFolder 1.2
IsObject 1.0	ReplaceCharSet 1.0
KillRes 1.4	ResolveAlias 1.1
LaunchDoc 1.0	ResText 1.4
LineCount 1.7	ScrapXCMDs 1.9
ListComponents 1.0	SelectDir 1.1
ListLogic 1.6	SelectFile 1.0
Listoid 3.0	SendPS 1.4
ListSelect 4.8	SetFileFlag 1.2
MacType 1.3	SetFinderLock 1.2
Menu 2.1	SetFInfo 1.0
Menu -2	SetMode 1.2
Mousoid 1.1	Set 1.1
NameNewFile 1.0	ShowHideFolder 1.2
Notification 1.0	SoundRecord 1.7
NubusList 1.0	StripDup 1.1
PictFile 1.7	StrWidth 1.0
PictToClip 1.4	Switch 1.3

5

Tabloid 1.1   WindName 1.1

Textoid 3.9   XRef 1.31

TextRes 1.4

X Marks the Spot

These are commands that I find myself using often:

- **SoundRecord** is a great way to get sounds into your Mac via the built-in microphone. I once made an impressive kiosk-based voice mail system using just this XCMD.

- **FileSharingMaster** gives your stacks total control over System 7's File Sharing. You can turn sharing on or off for the entire machine or just a particular folder, or look up the list of users and groups.

- **Calendoid** puts a by-month calendar in a floating window.

- **ArchiveContent** returns a list of the contents of a given Compactor Pro archive. Wanna make a diskette organizer? This could play a key part.

Try it, you'll like it. I'm sure you'll find your own favorites.

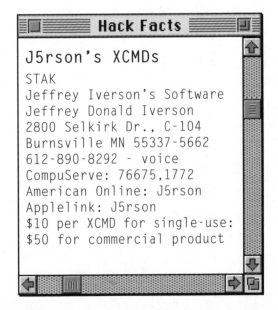

```
═══ Hack Facts ═══

J5rson's XCMDs
STAK
Jeffrey Iverson's Software
Jeffrey Donald Iverson
2800 Selkirk Dr., C-104
Burnsville MN 55337-5662
612-890-8292 - voice
CompuServe: 76675,1772
American Online: J5rson
Applelink: J5rson
$10 per XCMD for single-use:
$50 for commercial product
```

This is one of the largest XCMD collections I've seen from a single individual. And next to Frederic Rinaldi's, it's the best presented and documented. Every external comes with good docs and and an on-screen example, so you can try it out. Plus, the license fee is spelled out in no uncertain terms, as Figure 5-6 shows.

Luckily for Jeffrey, unluckily for you, most of these XCMDs aren't very complicated. For the most part, they inquire as to the state of the system and return a TRUE or FALSE. This can be handy if you need to know some specific system information.

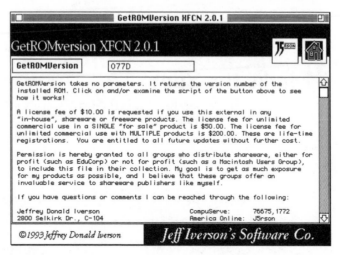

Figure 5-6. *The licensing terms for Jeffrey Iverson's XCMDs*

Some of Jeffrey's XCMDs are superfluous. For instance, GetFileExists returns a TRUE if the given file is on the hard drive. Well, HyperCard will already do that. But for those other programs that use HyperCard XCMDs (such as FoxBase or MicroPhone II), these seemingly redundant externals can be lifesavers.

but, then again, when in a HyperCard stack will you ever need to know if virtual memory is turned on? Or why would you care what the TrueType outline mode is? I suppose there are obscure yet entirely valid reasons, so thank God that Jeffrey's done this work for us. These are some of his handier XCMDs:

- **GetFileCopy**, which (despite its odd name) copies a file.
- **Play AIFF**, which plays an AIFF-format sound file.
- **SpeakString**, which uses Apple's Speech Manager (a text-to-speech synthesis system) to read the string aloud. This in and of itself is no great feat, there being a bazillion other XCMDs for this, but Jeffrey also includes GetSpeechBusy, which tells you if the Speech Manager is still saying something. Cool! Otherwise, you might speak

two words at the same time, and I think we all know how painful that can be.

X Marks the Spot

Jeffrey has been a busy boy. Here's a list of all the XCMDs he has created. Since there are so many, and since most of the names are self-explanatory, I won't bother writing a description of each.

d'Eject XCMD 1.0.1

FlushEvents XCMD 1.0.1

Gestalt XFCN 4.1.1

Get/SetCreateDate 2.0.1

Get/SetCreator 3.0.1

Get/SetInvisible 2.0.1

Get/SetModDate 1.0.1

Get/SetNameLock 2.0.1

Get/SetStationery 2.0.1

GetA/UXVersion XFCN 2.0.1

GetAddressingMode XFCN 2.0.1

GetAliasManager XFCN 2.0.1

GetAppleEvents XFCN 2.0.1

GetAppleTalk XFCN 2.0.1

GetApplication XFCN 1.0.1

GetCapsLock XFCN 1.0.1

GetConnectionManager XFCN 2.0.1

GetCRM XFCN 2.0.1

GetCTBVersion XFCN 2.0.1

GetDBAccessManager XFCN 2.0.1

GetDITLExtensions XFCN 2.0.1

GetEasyAccess XFCN 2.0.1

GetEditionManager XFCN 2.0.1

GetEjectable XFCN 2.0.1

GetFileCopy XCMD 1.0.1

GetFileExists XFCN 1.0.1

GetFileSystemMgr XFCN 2.0.1

GetFileTransferMgr XFCN 2.0.1

GetFindFolder XFCN 2.0.1

GetFontManager XFCN 2.0.1

GetFPUType XFCN 2.0.1

GetFreeK XFCN 2.0.1

GetGestaltVersion XFCN 2.0.1

GetHardware XFCN 2.0.1

GetHelpManager XFCN 2.0.1

GetKeyboard XFCN 2.0.1

GetLocalVolumes XFCN 2.0.1

GetLogicalPageSize XFCN 2.0.1

GetLogicalRAMSize XFCN 2.0.1	GetScriptMgr XFCN 2.0.1
GetLowMemorySize XFCN 2.0.1	GetSerialMgr XFCN 2.0.1
GetMachine XFCN 2.0.1	GetSIZE XFCN 2.0.1
GetMacName XFCN 1.0.1	GetSound XFCN 2.0.1
GetMiscellaneous XFCN 2.0.1	GetSpeechBusy XFCN 1.0.1
GetMMU XFCN 2.0.1	GetSpeechManager XFCN 1.0.1
GetMonitors XFCN 1.2.1	GetStandardFile XFCN 2.0.1
GetNotificationMgr XFCN 2.0.1	GetStandardNBP XFCN 2.0.1
GetOS XFCN 2.0.1	GetSystemVersion XFCN 2.0.1
GetOStable XFCN 2.0.1	GetTermManager XFCN 2.0.1
GetOutlineMethod XFCN 1.0.1	GetTextEdit XFCN 2.0.1
GetOwnerName XFCN 1.0.1	GetThreadManager XFCN 1.0.1
GetParity XFCN 2.0.1	GetTimeManager XFCN 2.0.1
GetPhysicalRAM XFCN 2.0.1	GetToolbox XFCN 2.0.1
GetPopUp XFCN 2.0.1	GetVirtualMemory XFCN 2.0.1
GetPopUpMenu XFCN 1.0.1	GetVolumes XFCN 1.0.1
GetPowerManager XFCN 2.0.1	MakeAlias XCMD 1.0.1
GetProcesses XFCN 2.0.1	PlayAIFF XCMD 1.0.1
GetProcessor XFCN 2.0.1	ScreenSize XFCN 1.2.1
GetQuickDraw XFCN 2.0.1	SetDate XCMD 3.0.1
GetResourceList XFCN 1.0.1	SetGlobal XCMD 3.0.1
GetResourceMgr XFCN 2.0.1	SetLock XCMD 2.2.1
GetROMsize XFCN 2.0.1	SpeakString XCMD 1.0.1
GetROMVersion XFCN 2.0.1	Unmounter XCMD 2.0.1
GetScriptCount XFCN 2.0.1	WipeOut XCMD 2.0.1

5

One Caveat

Jeffrey's XCMDs come in a StuffIt archive. There is one stack per XCMD. This might lead the less generous folk among us to wonder why Jeff just didn't upload his XCMDs individually, so that one could pick and choose online and save the download charges for a package so big. But we're not that petty, are we?

Gone Commercial

You can squeak by using only shareware and freeware externals, but keep in mind that there's a large number of cool externals for sale.

Heizer Software has a catalog of cool tools for HyperCard programmers. You can get WindowScript—a tool for creating window (and even complete) user-interfaces from within HyperCard. Or CompileIt—which takes your HyperTalk commands and compiles them into externals. (Yes! The easy way to make externals.) Or ColorIt—complete color control of your stacks. And that's just the beginning of the list.

They sell more than HyperCard tools, too. Definitely worth checking out. Give them a call at 510-943-7667 and ask for their latest catalog.

OSAX and the Single Hacker

AppleScript is Apple's totally hot new scripting language. You can write scripts that work with certain applications. It's system-wide, so that you can control many different applications simultaneously.

Cool as it is, the command set is profoundly limited. There's very little in the way of native commands in AppleScript. It's easy to extend the AppleScript command set, however: just use an OSAX. An *OSAX* is an external command for AppleScript. Believe it or not, most of the commands you'd expect to be built into the AppleScript language are actually in OSAXes. ("Like what?" you ask. How about things like, oh, addition and subtraction? String handling? Variable coercion? Pretty crazy, huh?)

Note

For some bizarre reason (mostly having to do with trendy cuteness I fear) the plural form of OSAX is generally known as OSAXen. Use whatever term you're comfortable with. I have to be trendy and cute, since it's in my contract.

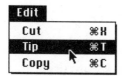

In Case You Were Wondering...IMHO= In My Humble Opinion. (Don't you get e-mail? Sheesh.)

But this means that OSAXen can do almost anything. Open windows, create files, make menus, play sounds—you name it, and an OSAX can do it. There has been a proliferation of cool OSAXen ever since the first version of AppleScript came out.

(This flood is not nearly proportional to the number of users working with AppleScript. What does this mean? There's a really dedicated core of hackers using this stuff. This is always a sign that something will soon explode.)

IMHO, AppleScript represents the future of programming—using higher-level languages as tools to do real programs. OSAXen are the bridge between the traditional C world and the realm of AppleScript. Below you'll find one of the best collections of OSAXen for AppleScript. I heartily recommend that you download these and try them out.

Since the art of OSAXing is fairly new, I was surprised to find a solid and mature collection of OSAXen already existed. Greg Quinn has done a fantastic job of creating OSAXen for every conceivable need.

I found Greg's collection on AppleLink, inside the AppleScript discussion folder. If you write AppleScripts, you'll want to hang out there as much as possible. This is the secret source of the Nile, the hidden Fountain of Youth, the scripting lounge of your dreams,

5

where any scripting question is answered quickly, and usually by a member of the AppleScript team to boot.

Power chitchat

Many of Greg's OSAXen provide a way to control PowerTalk, which is part of System 7 Pro. Most users don't have PowerTalk yet. Many people have preconceived biases against it. I know I do. It clutters up my desktop with five new icons. Heck, I can do that without any help from system software! But we need to relax and see what new capabilities PowerTalk can give us. And with these PowerTalk OSAXen, I'm sure we can put a cool, human face on it no matter how hideously Apple has screwed it up.

Greg's OSAX collection offers some unique functionality. Among the commands that improve PowerTalk, some track down information about the monitors (as shown in Figure 5-7), play QuickTime movies and sounds, or even let you switch the active printer. Of all these, I have my favorites:

- **Is Application Running** lets you know if an application has already been opened. This is great to use before sending a Quit command to an application. (Think about

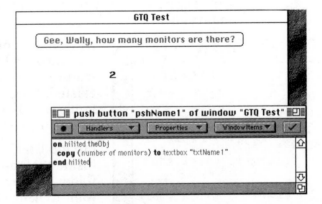

Figure 5-7.　*In this AppleScript application I created, clicking on the button will return the number of monitors currently connected to the Macintosh*

it. If it's not already open, the application is opened, just so it can then quit. Silly.)

- **Request Attention** provides support for the Notification Manager. This has been badly needed by scripters forever. With this OSAX, a script can perform a time-consuming task in the background and then let the user know it's finished by placing a small icon in the menu bar. Very handy, especially if you've written scripts to watch for special e-mail or flag downloaded files for key words.

- **Omit** bridges the biggest hole in AppleScript: the lack of a delete function. Believe it or not, there is no way to delete things in AppleScript. For instance, if you had a list of stuff such as {"Ham", "Turkey", "Swiss", "Rye" and wanted to delete the "Rye" (I know how you feel), you can't. But if you had the Omit OSAX and the string "Ham,Turkey,Swiss,Rye" you could just say

```
Omit in "Ham,Turkey,Swiss,Rye" at 17 for 4
```

You would get this: and Rye would be gone

```
"Ham,Turkey,Swiss"
```

which is all the chow you really need.

Greg Brady – Surfboard + AppleScript = Greg Quinn? You Decide!

Below is the full list of Greg Quinn's OSAXen. Since he did such a bang-up job of naming them, I won't describe them in detail. Suffice it to say, I can't recommend them more highly. I use these OSAXen every day both at work and at home. I'm sure you will too.

Address of	Available Dialects
Application Info for	Choose Address

Choose from List	Number of Sounds
Choose Link	Offsets of
Current Date in Seconds	Omit
Current Dialect	Play Movie in
Date String for	Play (Sound)
Depth	Record Sound to
Does Monitor Support Depth	Relocate
Front Application	Remove
Get User	Rename
Index of (monitor)	Request Attention
Is Application Running	Set Printer to
List Applications	Sharing Information
List Links	Sort
List Nodes	String to Application Coercion Handler
List Zones	Switch to Launcher
Mail To	This Application
Make Alias	Time String for
Number of Monitors	Version of

Greg Quinn's OSAX collection includes a great documentation file, which offers many scripting samples. Plus, it also comes with a folder filled with scripting examples, which you can open and examine in the Script Editor (or even just use as is. The drag-and-drop printer idea he includes is very cool.)

If you do any AppleScripting at all, make sure you grab this collection. It's available on AppleLink (Developer Services:AppleScript Discussion:OSAX Swap), or you can probably locate it on the Internet.

Coming Up Next—Building with Blocks

That about wraps up our discussion of external code add-ons for HyperCard. I hope you learned that HyperCard, AppleScript, and other scripting environments offer great functionality and flexibility when coupled with external commands, and that it all comes much easier than writing in traditional programming languages.

Speaking of traditional programming languages, we're next going to delve into the world of shareware programming languages for the Macintosh. We'll look at some mainstream stuff, as well as alternative languages—sort of the computer equivalent of Esperanto. So if you're stuck in a C rut, this is the chance to cut loose with that dusty LISP you learned in college!

5

Ciphers and Secret Messages: Programming Languages

Back in the Renaissance, if memory serves, the language one spoke served more purpose than just inquiring directions to the nearest outhouse from the closest serf. For certain groups of people—usually royal types—the language spoken at any given time had more to do with diplomacy—a concern for what was appropriate—than simple communication. Why else would a Czar speak French? Because, silly, French was the, and I do mean *the*, language of cultured types all over the dragon-sprinkled globe. Want to make the finest clocks of the post-middle ages? Then you would have been best off speaking German. Want to hang around the cathedrals, appearing religious and smart? Learn Latin. See?

Nothing is true. Everything is permitted.

—William S.Burroughs

In this respect, the computer world is strangely similar to the multilingual silliness played out at Renaissance festivals. Computer languages, like their aural counterparts, have their appropriate niches. Where parlez-ing in French would be appropriate for some powdered aesthete, an equally pale computer jock who wanted to write artificial intelligence programs would chat with an electronic pal in Lisp. Why? Is

Lisp that much better than other languages for AI work? Partially. But it only got that way out of tradition. Lisp is what people use for AI work. Same with French. French was not inherently better for discussing culture, but after all these years of tradition and association, I'll be damned if I find someone who doesn't think that French sounds at least a little artsy.

Oh, there's more. Computer languages have histories behind them as well; external factors that formed them into what they are today. Just as Eskimos have many words for snow because they needed words to describe a major part of their environment, Forth is fast and lean because it was used originally in the tiny computers used by astronomers to control telescopes.

And your darling little Mac is more than cosmopolitan enough to chat easily in many, many of these different tongues. In fact, if your Mac were human, it's smooth delivery of any language would enable it to pick up anybody it wanted to at any party, impressing the swooning prey with *bon mots* from varied tongues, and peppering its conversation with the mysterious and seductive accents of a well-designed graphical interface.

To be a programmer, you've got to write code in some language, and the Mac universe contains many wonderful yet little-known programming environments. We're going to look at some environments for doing real work in the Forth, C, and Lisp programming languages.

Go Forth Young Lad

I'm not sure why, but Forth is a terribly popular Macintosh shareware programming language. As far as I can tell, Forth never quite cut it in the real world—the few folks who made

Forth interpreters have either gone out of business, or are fighting for recognition in a jaded C marketplace.

Kriya Systems had one of the earliest programming languages for the Macintosh. Called Neon, it offered a fast object-oriented Forth interpreter. Back then, no one knew what object-oriented meant—I thought it referred to kleptomania, myself.

Well, after a while Apple got all serious about object-oriented programming, and Larry Tessler at *MacWorld* started talking about Classcal and MacApp, and object-oriented anything became hot. Everyone whipped up an object-oriented version of their language, and Neon was left in the dust.

Quote

Once you are informed—and have started to inform others—you must start acting. Knowledge without action produces demoralization.
—John A. Stormer, None Dare Call It Treason

6

Neon Fades On

Neon—or, more accurately, its progeny, MOPS and Yerk—is totally cool. IMHO, they exceed the promise of object-oriented C or Pascal. Unfortunately, you're not going to find many employers who will make the switch to a weird, halfway-supported shareware language. And who can blame them for resisting the temptation, since if you're using the language for mission-critical apps, it helps to have tools with a track record and tech support (although Symantec's recent efforts at tech support make shareware look more and more attractive).

But if you're in this for yourself, if you find your bliss hacking at your Mac for sheer enlightenment and enjoyment, you could do much worse than to play with these languages.

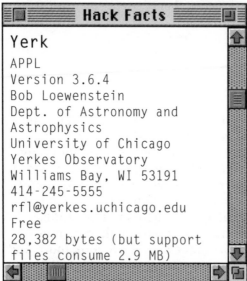

MOPS and Yerk are so similar, it's frightening. Both are based on the Neon Forth engine. At startup, they look nearly identical. In fact, if you look at the manuals for both you'll swear one was copied from the other with minimal changes, like some junior-high-schooler's homework.

Both programs have been tweaked on a low level, and offer some interesting twists from the original neon. For example, both products can do early or late binding, depending on what you'd prefer. This wasn't a feature of the original Neon.

The differences lie in the library of classes and the quality of support that is available, as well as the future direction of the products. I'm not a Forth guru, so I asked around. If you want to choose between them, use these guidelines:

- Many experienced users think Yerk has the more complete class library. MOPS is smaller and more compact. But both class libraries are terribly complete and well-documented.

- Yerk's interpreter lets you try out program snippets as you go, as Figure 6-1, shows. (Note that the code shown in Figure 6-1, which draws a few boxes in a window, would produce the same output if used in MOPS.)

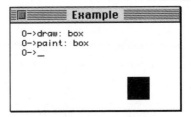

Figure 6-1. *Code to try painting and drawing in Yerk*

- Both products are supported by a core group of dedicated hackers. There's no company behind their efforts. There's no tech-support phone line, but you can e-mail questions to the authors.

- Both products are in the public domain. The hackers who support each system are responsible for the future direction of the products. Yerk is maintained by the University of Chicago, which uses Yerk for some internal development efforts. MOPS is maintained by Michael Hore and a group of very dedicated people.

So which do you pick? It's a mixed bag in my book. You can use either to create commercial software. Download them both and try them out. Read the manuals. You can pick up the basic concepts of Forth in a few minutes, and be doing some neat programming within a day. It's worthwhile if you program for a living. Stretch your mind, why don't you?

Word up

Here's a quote from Michael Hore's Mops manual:

"My hope is that over a period of time, Mops users will, by sharing their developments, contribute to the ongoing Mops effort. As a one-man, very part-time operation, I can't hope by myself to compete with all the commercial outfits producing gigantic, all-singing, all-dancing development systems for the Mac. I would be happy to concentrate on the low-level implementation of the Mops nucleus and basic system code."

I couldn't have put it better myself (without my ghostwriters, that is). This is the way to give back to the shareware community: create cool code objects that do wonderful and sorely needed things, and share these code objects with everyone else. Give back to that great yawning shareware maw.

```
Hack Facts

PocketForth
APPL
Version 6.3
Chris Heilman
PO Box 8345
Phoenix AZ 85066-8345
CompuServe: 70566,1474
America Online: cheilman
15,476 bytes
```

PocketForth epitomizes the Forth language: its small, lean, mean, and fast. Unlike MOPS and YERK, which utilize object-oriented extensions to the Forth language and offer class libraries to boot, PocketForth provides a minimalist Forth interpreter with only the basic Forth functions.

This isn't to say that you can't write advanced software in PocketForth. In fact, PocketForth provides support for all of the Mac toolbox calls, in addition to floating-point SANE math and a standard Forth function set.

You can send and receive Apple Events; you can draw graphics and text in color; you can even make your compiled Forth program a drag-and-drop application. There's nothing shabby about this Forth.

All of this in 16k! Well, not really; the dictionary files can be larger, and you'll most likely need to load at least some of the dictionaries. The sample programs make it easy to learn Forth as you go. This is a great beginners Forth; a wonderful and inexpensive way to get started in a new language.

It also comes in a DA version, so you can run it under System 6 as a DA. This was essential back in the days when memory was limited and System 6 ruled. Even nowadays, I can use the small DA on my PowerBook 100 and still have enough memory left over to multitask.

Lisp

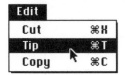

When using PowerLisp, save early, save often.

OK. On the one hand, you have Forth, a language designed to have a tiny executable size and low memory requirement. On the other hand, you have Lisp, which is designed for extensive and easy list processing—the upshot of which is that it eats memory and processor cycles like a cop eats donuts.

Lisp is the teacher's pet language of the artificial-intelligence and natural-language-processing crowd. I've been playing with a natural-language system someone built in Apple's MCL, and it's very cool: I can type English statements and have it interpret them. It's also rather uncool in that it takes 30 MB of RAM and a Quadra 840AV to run at a respectable speed.

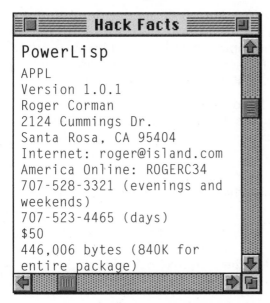

Hack Facts

PowerLisp
APPL
Version 1.0.1
Roger Corman
2124 Cummings Dr.
Santa Rosa, CA 95404
Internet: roger@island.com
America Online: ROGERC34
707-528-3321 (evenings and weekends)
707-523-4465 (days)
$50
446,006 bytes (840K for entire package)

The first thing you notice about PowerLisp is its user interface (see Figure 6-2). Of all the shareware programming products I've seen, this has the most professional and complete user interface by far. The next thing you notice is its speed—it compiles to native 680x0 code. It's blazing.

The next thing you may notice is, you've crashed into the debugger. At least I did. I crashed a couple of times while getting to know this program. Be prepared to save often and use your reset switch.

PowerLISP conforms to the Common Lisp standard, which is like the ANSI library standard for C. You can rely on a set of common functions, predefined in the language and available for your use. Generally, the functions are things like string manipulations and file handling, but they don't stop there. The Common Lisp standard is fairly massive—you'll want to check out a book to learn more.

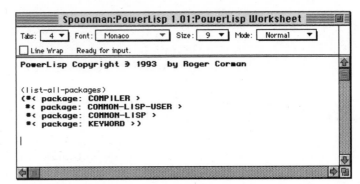

Figure 6-2. *PowerLISP offers simple control over the display of programs. Remember, use the* ENTER *key, not the* RETURN *key*

The libraries that come with PowerLISP aren't compiled. They come as text files, and they are interpreted as needed. To speed things up, you can compile them yourself by executing the file "compile-libraries.lisp". If you're doing more than just playing with PowerLISP, I recommend this highly.

PowerLISP uses a built-in editor called PowerEdit. PowerEdit does some very cool things. I wish other Mac programming environments did just some of this stuff (hint, hint Symantec):

- When you drag the scroll bar thumb, the text scrolls interactively. No more hunting for the right portion of your source code!

- Text font and size, as well as tab stops, can be set in the editor from the menus at the top of the window. These settings are stored in the resource fork of each file, so they stick between sessions.

- Comments are displayed in italics, and any text the interpreter gives back to you is displayed in bold.

If you've ever had any interest in Lisp, PowerLISP is the best way to get that bug out of your butt. Apple's MCL costs $300, consumes a huge amount of hard disk space, and doesn't have an editor that's nearly as cool.

Swimming in the Shareware C

It's not the size of the dog in the fight, but the size of the fight in the dog
—Terry Robbins, Weather Underground

You know how I feel about C. Yet C remains the most popular programming language around today. You can't spit in a bookstore without hitting an array of books on C programming. (Actually, you can't spit in a bookstore without getting arrested.) C is available for all kinds of computers, and to some degree source code is platform independent. People from all walks of life have written programs in C and lived to tell the tale. So I just need to relax, right?

Despite my grave personal misgivings about this—I think C should be banned and I think Kernighan & Ritchie should be fed to the sharks—I will now discuss a couple of generally available freeware C compilers. Both GCC and GNU are available on the Internet at the info-mac archive (FTP to sumex-aim.stanford.edu) in the /dev directory.

6

Note

Keep in mind that I don't recommend using these, and it has nothing to do with my loathing of C. If you're writing programs, doubtless you'll want to give them to people. If you give your programs to people, you'll want them to not crash. If you want them to not crash, you want a compiler you can trust. And as of right now, trusting a shareware C compiler not to crash is a little like hopping a seat on the training flights at Air Bangladesh.

"Shut your steakcatcher," I can hear you yelling. Okay, okay, enough of my pontificating, it's on to the programs.

```
═══════════ Hack Facts ═══════════
GCC
MPST (Macintosh
Programmer's Workshop Tool)
TEXT (Source code files)
Version 1.37.1r14
Apple Computer, Inc. and
the Free Software
Foundation, Inc.
Free
```

GCC is a high-quality C and C++ compiler that was developed by Apple's Advanced Technology Group for some internal project they were working on. They decided to release it to the world at large, albeit without any support.

This compiler is the GNU C compiler (GCC, get it?) The GNU project of the Free Software Foundation is working to create freely available clones of the UNIX operating system, the PostScript page-description language, and the C++ programming language. GCC belongs to the C++ effort.

This compiler runs under MPW (Macintosh Programmer's Workshop), and works just like Apple's MPW C compiler. You enter commands in the Worksheet window to compile your programs, or you can execute makefiles. GCC can simply replace the standard MPW C you've been using.

The compiler cleverly translates source code into an internal language called RTL (Register Transfer Language). From there, it compiles the RTL code into machine-dependent assembly language. This scheme was chosen so that the compiler could make highly optimized object code for any target microprocessor.

The benefits are clear: it's a simple matter to write programs for a wide range of machines. The same source file can be cross-compiled to work on Macs, UNIX machines, Windows boxes, and so on. The list of target machines you can port to is embarrassingly long.

Portly listing

Here's the list of processors you can port your GCC code to:

3b1, a29k, aix385, alpha, altos3068, amix, arm, convex, crds, elxsi, fx2800, fx80, genix, hp320, clipper, Intel 386 (running under DOS, isc, sco, sysv.3, sysv.4, mach, bsd, linux, windows, or OS/2), iris, i860, i960, irix4, m68k, m88ksvsv.3, mips-news, mot3300, next, ns32k,

*nws3250-v.4, hp-pa, pc532, plexus, pyramid, romp,
rs6000, sparc-sunos, sparc-solaris2, sparc-sysv.4, spur,
sun386, tahoe, tow, umpis, vax-vms, vax-bsd, we32k,
hitachi-(SH,8300)*

*I found this list on the Internet in comp.sys.mac.programmer.
Many thanks to Jacques Marcoux who posted it
(<esrilcmc.aes.doe.CA!jmarcoux>). Please note that
Macintosh falls under the "m68k" category.*

I don't recommend using GCC on the Mac. Why? Well, once again, it's unsupported software. Apple doesn't lay claim to it and won't support it. And Freesoft hates all things Apple, and in fact they ask folks to boycott Apple products, so I doubt they would be very much help.

Also, you need more than this package to get started. You'll need to purchase MPW (Macintosh Programmer's Workshop, Apple's editing and building environment) from APDA. You'll also need to buy Apple's MPW C compiler. Huh? Yeah, you see, GCC doesn't come with any C libraries, so you'll need to scarf them from Apple's official C. So, you end up saving no money over buying the official Apple thing outright.

I GNU you could

Believe it or not, there actually are people even more altruistic than shareware authors.

The Free Software Foundation, Inc., the inventors of GCC and everything prefixed with a "GNU," gives away all of its source code. All of it. Everything. For all of its products. And you can use it in any way, in any project you're working on. But there's one small catch: your own source code must be equally available to your users.

It's what some call a "copyleft" (as opposed to a copyright). You own the portions of your code that you write yourself. Anything else that you borrowed from the GNU stuff, you must make freely available to your users.

It's a clever idea, and it strikes back at the same software licensing issues that make me kick and scream. If everyone

6

has source code, then everyone is free to fix bugs or make incremental changes or simply rip off good ideas. (This assumes that all computer users are programmers, which is no longer a safe assumption.) The Freesoft Company is interested in the spreading of good ideas.

"The word free doesn't refer to price; it refers to freedom."
　　　　—Richard Stallman, *president of the Free Software Foundation.*

Naturally no companies use GNU products for anything real. I mean, corporations have to make huge investments in their code. They're not going to hand it out to just anyone. Even at the small company I work at, source code is a jealously guarded secret.

I shouldn't say nobody—lots of people actually use GNU products every day. Many real programmers use it to develop great software, and they simply include their source code (or make it available on the Internet at an FTP site). It's just that corporations—with so much to hide and so much to lose—wouldn't get caught dead in a GNU license.

Secrets aside, Freesoft is after bigger fish. They're out to change the world, and they're liable to do it.

Unless you have a compelling reason to use GCC—like a huge body of existing work in GNU C for another platform that you want to port to the Mac—I would use something else.

Hack Facts

Harvest C

APPL
Version 1.3
Eric W. Sink
3101 Amy Dr.
Champaign, IL 61821
esink@spyglass.com
Free
2,034,309 bytes for entire folder

Mac folk don't take kindly to command-line interfaces and cryptic commands; or else we'd all still be using an Atari 512st. That's a problem with Apple's MPW environment: it's got all the power of a scripting language, with all the typing, memorization, and headaches of a scripting language.

Harvest C follows in the footsteps of the Think C compiler from Symantec. It has the same project-based metaphor, in which one window lists all of the files in a project; these are the source code files that will become your compiled application. In fact, many of Harvest C's menu commands echo resoundingly from Think C so if you've used that compiler, you won't have any conceptual hurdles here. Harvest C's Project window also is reminiscent of Think C, as Figure 6-3 shows. The Project window lists all of the files used; double-clicking a file will launch it in a (not-included) text editor.

Since it uses the GCC compiler, the compiler code is available and is reusable in your own projects under the same GNU copyleft.

The compiler itself is the GCC compiler. In version 1.2 of Harvest C, the compiler was based on Eric Sink's own experiments in compiler design. In the ReadMe file, Eric claims that it was one hell of a learning process, and he seems vaguely embarrassed by the code it generated. In addition, he had trouble tracking down various compiler code-generation bugs, so he switched to the GCC compiler in this version.

Since it uses the GCC compiler, you'll still need to get the header files from Apple (although, thankfully, Eric gives full contact information for getting the goods from APDA; it's only $40 for the headers alone on a floppy).

I've asked around on the net about Harvest C, and the general consensus seems to be that, while a neat idea, it's

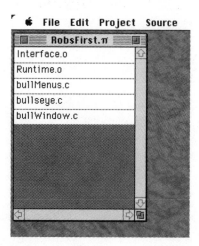

Figure 6-3. *Check out the menus—they'll be familiar to any Think C user.*

nowhere near commercial quality, even with the GCC compiler. Most people would like to see it improved; many of the bugs listed in the early ReadMe files remain, and Eric says that he doesn't have the time required to tackle the all-consuming project of perfecting Harvest C.

Should you get this? If you're a C nut, definitely. It's worth playing with and experimenting with. Remember to report any and all bugs to the author, (and don't be a jerk about it, either; he's got a day job too).

Coming Up Next: Putting the Pieces Together

If being fluent in the right programming language is an important part of writing good code, then keeping a well-stocked library of objects and classes is a little like building up your vocabulary. Knowing the rudiments of the language will help you get by, but you'll never impress, amaze, charm, and delight the natives unless you toss in a few SAT vocabulary hummers.

In Chapter 7, we'll examine some powerful object and class libraries that can save you tons of time and effort, and in the process make you appear slick and sophisticated.

Object Libraries, Class Libraries, and You

When I was a kid, some of my favorite toys were Lego building blocks. I loved them. My first set was this really old one that had huge blocks. My later sets were even better. I had a moon-base Lego set that had (in addition to the standard types of Lego blocks) these special pieces shaped like rocket nozzles, radar dishes, hinges, seats—you name it. As I got more sets, I found within each one some great new development in Lego-piece technology—a distinct piece that solved a given building problem perfectly—and so I replaced my clumsy ersatz radar dishes and hinges and nozzles (crudely formed out of discolored, blocky Legos) with more specialized pieces that allowed me to create more and more complex objects with far less hassle and frustration. It was . . . . sublime.

for me, programming has been reminiscent of those early Lego productions. My first attempts at programming were rather inefficient and clunky affairs, relying often on brute force over elegance. Then, object-oriented programming came around.

Hoola OOPs

For those of you who've spent too much time in your basement programming an AI brain for your solar-powered mechanical dog-bot pet substitute, object-oriented programming involves writing programs in a language that has been specifically designed to use an object—a chunk of a program that contains both data and function.

Object-oriented programming (or OOP) was a new approach—I could write programs and incorporate my rare well-written sections of code into other programs. So, if I had this really great sorting algorithm (yeah, as if), I could put it into an *object* (which is just a chunk of a program that contains both data and functions) and plug that object in wherever it was needed. What I realized is that these programming objects are just special pieces—the computer equivalent of, say, that swiveling right-angle Lego piece. You could achieve the same effect with regular blocks, but not nearly as easily, quickly, or efficiently.

Object-oriented programming is the only way to go these days. Objects make your programming life simpler and easier. And they are the perfect way to share code with fellow programmers. In this chapter, we'll look at some of the best objects around.

Object-oriented programming, with its independently mobile sections of code, has another great advantage. Other people, with more experience than you, can make really clever hunks of code that, eventually, you or I can use to make massively cool programs. That's what I plan to show you in this chapter.

even
if you don't use an object-oriented programming language, you're still covered in this chapter. You'll learn about neat code libraries. A *code library* is something that you just drop into your project and use; it requires little knowledge or understanding of what goes on

under the hood. Very cool and highly useful. We'll look at these libraries specifically:

- **Toolbar manager** creates Microsoft-style toolbars for any program you write.
- **SpriteWorld** is a set of routines that can be used to create high-speed color games.
- **TE32K** breaks the 32K limit on the Mac's built-in TextEdit.

Living in Object Poverty

The terminology can get confusing, so I want to be very clear about what we're talking about. As noted earlier, an object is a chunk of a program that contains both data and functions. Generally, the data is private to an object, but the object's functions can be called by outside forces.

For instance, in the Think Class Library, a CWindow is an object that implements a standard Macintosh window. It keeps private data such as the window's height and width. It has functions that allow you to activate, deactivate, move, resize, or close the window. This object is known as a *class*.

what we're looking at here are classes created by folks and distributed as freeware or shareware. For instance, Joe Zobkiw distributes his CMoviePlayer class via the net; you can download it, add it to your program's existing classes, compile it with your program, and play QuickTime movies with generally a few lines of code.

Object libraries refer to something totally different. The word object in this case refers to object code, which is the end result of source code. Object code is what comes out of a compiler.

Object code libraries are basically a set of procedures or functions that someone has written and offered to let you use. Unlike with a class, you don't get the source code; what

*It is a veritable
wonder that we can
carry out this
business without
getting into the
greatest difficulties.
—Albert Einstein*

you get is precompiled and ready to run. You simply add it to your project, and leave it to your language's linker to worry about the hows and whys of hooking in the code.

For instance, the SpriteWorld is a code object written in C. Since it's a precompiled code object, you can sling it into any project of your own. So if you're thinking about creating the next *Kung-Fu Nazi Bloodfeast* and need some way to display the cool color graphics you've made, you simply load the library into your project and let 'er rip.

Object code libraries tend to be easier to use, but object-oriented programming objects are pretty straightforward, too. It all depends on what you need, and the language you'll be using to write in. If you're not using Object Pascal or C++, then object-oriented stuff would be as useful as a dentist at a wedding. (Which means not very useful, folks. Must I explain everything?)

The ROM Maze

Ever since day one, the biggest complaint about programming the Macintosh was the complexity of its ROMs. I can remember a comment in *St. Mac* magazine issue #3 (yes, *St. Mac*—published by the beloved *Softalk Apple II* magazine—now I am definitely showing my age) along the lines of "we expected lots more software to be out by now, but looking at the book *Inside Macintosh*, we understand it's an undertaking." At that point *Inside Macintosh* was already so big Apple had to get a company that usually printed phone books to print it. (I've still got one: it's a real collector's item.) And that was in 1984. *Inside Macintosh* has grown to six volumes, plus specialized manuals for QuickTime, PowerTalk, and so on.

Object-oriented programming isn't perfect

The problem with object-oriented languages is the wretched complexity involved in learning the class libraries needed to use the languages. Class libraries are generally functionally complete and wonderful to use, but miserable to learn.

In the early days of programming, a program was a very linear sequence of instructions to the machine. Then along came procedural programming, which is both an art and a science. Procedures can be used to hide the complexities and break the program down into logical units.

In object-oriented programming, objects hide data and instructions inside themselves. This is both a blessing and a curse. The blessing is that they are little robots that you tell what to do and don't need to know how they are built or how their mechanics were created. The curse is that what you gain in ease of use, you lose in control.

Have you ever closed your eyes, held your arms out to your sides, and then tried to touch your fingers together without looking? Well, making links with objects that you can't delve into is about as easy. What do you do to change the font used in the Think Class Library, for example? Which object traps the command, and which carries it out? The problem has become one of scope.

The trend is to make smaller and smaller objects, but to build more complex combinations of objects. We're reducing the complexity of each individual object, but increasing the complexity of the relationship between objects.

This relationship between objects is very, very hard to describe visually. Look at our code browsers; they've become spiderwebs of interrelationships. Nowadays the hard part is figuring out how objects interact, and our existing tools don't work well for that.

I don't have an easy answer for this one, but I'm still a big disciple in the church of object-oriented programming. I wouldn't write a Mac application any other way. But it's getting harder and harder to work with our existing tools.

Interestingly, the brain works in a similar fashion. Each individual neuron is pretty stupid; it's the connections of neurons that have the real power. So maybe we're heading in the right direction. Then again, maybe our brains are as screwed up as object-oriented programming. A scary thought.

Suffice it to say, the learning curve for programming a Mac looks something like the Olympic ski-jumping ramp, only backward. It's a hell of a climb for folks just starting out. But luckily, there are some things out there to help you.

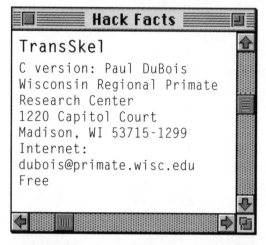

Hack Facts

TransSkel

C version: Paul DuBois
Wisconsin Regional Primate
Research Center
1220 Capitol Court
Madison, WI 53715-1299
Internet:
dubois@primate.wisc.edu
Free

Hack Facts

TransSkel

Pascal version: Owen
Hartnett
OHM Software Company
163 Richard Dr.
Tiverton, RI 02878
Internet: omh@cs.brown.edu
Free

TransSkel is an application framework. Basically, it provides a "skeleton" application that handles all the basics: dealing with the menu bar, opening and closing windows, tracking mousedowns in scrollbars, etc. In theory, all you have to do is put some meat on the skeleton, and voilà! Instant program.

It's not quite that simple, sadly. You still need to learn the real basics: about the resource manager and how resources work, what events are and what they mean, things like that. But these are the low-level basics.

For example, the TransSkel calls a routine of yours when a window is opened. You need to supply the routine to display stuff in that window.

I'd say if you have comfortably skimmed volume I of *Inside Macintosh*, and you have a vague understanding of it, dive into TransSkel and see what happens. Put SysBeeps in various places and find out how things work.

TransSkel can be a great learning tool, but it's also useful as a starting point for your own programming projects, no matter how experienced you are. Many veteran programmers on the Internet have told me they use TransSkel to jump-start their own applications.

It makes sense. Every time you write a Mac app you need to write the code to handle events, menu selections, and so on. You'll make a huge efficiency leap if you start reusing that code. And if you make a huge efficiency leap, think about the result: you can spend all that free time watching *The Simpsons* and *The Real World.*

One nice thing that TransSkel does is separate your application-specific code from its shell code. So you can compile the shell once and use it an infinite number of times. All you have to do for each new program is write the code that makes your new application unique.

TANSTAAFL, folks

No matter which application framework you use, you're gonna be stuck with a learning curve of some kind. (There Ain't No Such Thing As A Free Lunch.) Either you need to learn a bunch of stuff up front—in which case, you're not gaining much from the application framework—or you'll have to learn the dirty details later, when you want to modify the framework to do something unique and interesting.

Either way, you've got some learning ahead of you. But there's much less to learn when a framework is doing all the really hard stuff. And TransSkel is a nice framework.

The newest *final* version of TransSkel I could find was 2.6. There is a beta version numbered 3.03b that appears to implement some new features, but I have yet to find documentation of the changes and known bugs, so stick with the older version for now.

Custom Code Resources and You

Well, there's another way to add libraries of code to your program. The Macintosh ROMs support the standard menus, windows, and controls, but the ROMs also allow customizable versions of these same interface elements. So, for example, if you want to create a special kind of menu that displays a color palette for a paint program, you can make a customized menu definition. Another example of a custom menu definition is Mercutio.

Mercutio

MDEF
Version 1.1.4
Ramon M. Felciano
1326 Masonic Ave.
San Francisco, CA 94117
Internet
felciano@summit.stanford.edu
Applelink : SUMMIT
America Online : SUMMITDev
CompuServe : 76166,3627
Freeware

The computer has become a common denominator that knows no intellectual, political, or bureaucratic bounds.
—*Cliff Stoll*

On the Macintosh, menu items can have command-key equivalents. That is, when you press a letter key along with a command key, the Menu Manager treats it the same as when you use the mouse to invoke a menu item.

Many commercial applications use special menus that, in addition to command-key combinations, use shift- and option-command key combinations. How can you do that? The problem is, the Mac's menu manager doesn't deal with key combinations. It only traps the command key. If you press command-option and some other key, it wouldn't know or care.

Mercutio cares. Deeply. You can use Mercutio to create and use menus that use shift, option and command key combinations. The program is split into three parts:

- A custom MDEF that you copy into your program with ResEdit. This MDEF knows how to draw the shift- and option-command key symbols.

- A special font that has the shift and option characters.

- Some C and Pascal code that works just like the Toolbox's MenuKey, only it knows how to check for shift- and option-command key sequences.

So when you use Mercutio, it's pretty simple to make menus that use SHIFT-COMMAND-B for "Bold" or OPTION-COMMAND-F for "Bring to Front". It's also very easy to create some hideously unintuitive menus with Mercutio, so keep the user interface guidelines in mind as you use it.

There's also a few caveats: Mercutio uses standard menu resources, so you can create your menus in ResEdit or any other menu editor. To specify a shift- or option-command key, you set the "Condense" or "Expanded" text style for that menu item. These styles are ignored—in Mercutio's MDEF, no menu items can be drawn in the Condensed or Expanded style—but they are used as flags to indicate which key combination to display and watch for.

Seeking the Source

Another way you can flatten that learning curve is to learn from others' examples. Apple provides sample programs on its Developer CD-ROMs and at its FTP site, but sometimes you need more—or sometimes, the Apple-approved solution isn't enough. In those cases, you need to look for example code elsewhere.

one of my favorite pastimes is what I call code snarfing—stealing good bits of code from wherever I can. (I mean, legitimately borrowing legally available code, of course. Please don't steal code.) Whenever I come across a good bit on the Internet or America Online, I paste it into my special code scrapbook. What I look for are inspired solutions, elegant implementations, or just stuff I think I'll find handy someday.

The programs described next are good sources for snarfing. Look for them on the info-mac server at sumex-aim@stanford.edu, or in the Mac Developer's Forum on America Online. Also, keep a close eye on the alt.mac.sources newsgroup, and of course the comp.sys.mac.programmer newsgroup as well.

clut_fade 1.0

Ever wonder how games and screen savers do that cool smooth-as-silk fade-out and fade-in effect? Well, Andrew Welch shows you how. Jonas Englund added a demo application that shows the fader code in action. This

recently saved my butt on a project, so I highly recommend it. Note that it doesn't work in 16- or 24-bit color modes.

Huffman Example

This demonstrates how to use Huffman encoding, which is a type of compression. Watch out: this code doesn't show you how to do Huffman *de*coding! But it's still great for learning purposes.

LaunchFile XCMD Source

Writing external commands is a minor art of its own. You need your code to be small, quick, and global-variable free. This source code demonstrates how to create good externals in Pascal.

POV 3.0, RTrace 1.0

This provides great examples of ray tracing with Phong and Gourad shading, off-screen pixmaps, background processing.

PwrSwitcher

This control panel used to be popular freeware, but the author has stopped supporting it and has released the source code to the world. You can learn things like: how to make a control panel, how to switch between processes, how to watch for a particular keydown.

Trie Example

One step beyond binary trees, a *trie* is a data structure that holds repetitive data in a small amount of memory. Source code and data structures are easily reusable.

Writeswll Jr

This is an AppleEvent-callable spelling checker; it's good to read this code and see how to handle AppleEvent in general, and the Text Suite in particular.

Use that Usenet

I've already suggested a few newsgroups to watch for Mac programming tips and tricks, primarily comp.sys.mac.programmer. But before you jump out there and ask really innocent questions that bore and annoy the old-timers, it's smart to run a background check.

at the info-mac ftp site (sumex-aim@stanford.edu), you can download archives full of question-answer repartee called the Usenet Macintosh Programmer's Guide, UMPG for short. UMPG contains answers to the most common questions posted to the c.s.m.p newsgroup since 1988. It comes as a folder of 19 files in Microsoft Word format. Matthew Mora compiled the files, which were last updated in 1992. They cover specific Macintosh programming problems.

Also, you can get the comp.sys.mac.programmer FAQ (Frequently Asked Questions list) from the same ftp site. This list contains answers to more general questions, such as brands of compilers and good magazines to read. It is updated regularly and posted to the comp.sys.mac.programmer newsgroup. (We have included a copy of this FAQ in Appendix C. Check it out.)

The best way to use these files is to read them straight through, using your programmer's total recall to remember everything. (Ha!) The next best way is to use Microsoft Word's multi-file search. Word can search all of the files in a folder, so you can search for all instances of "copybits," for instance, and see everything anyone had to say on that topic.

7

```
┌─────────────────────────────────┐
│▤█▌▤▤▤▤▤ Hack Facts ▤▤▤▤█▌▤│
├─────────────────────────────────┤
│Toolbar manager              ⬆ │
│OBJ (Think Pascal code        ▒│
│library)                      ▒│
│SNR Enterprises               ▒│
│Narayan Sainaney              ▒│
│3480 Carnarvon Ave.           ▒│
│North Vancouver, BC, V7N 3K9  ▒│
│CANADA                        ▒│
│Free (see text)               ▒│
│97,780 bytes                  ⬇ │
├─────────────────────────────────┤
│⬅ ▒▒▒▓▒▒▒▒▒▒▒▒▒▒▒▒▒▒▒▒▒ ➡ ▣│
└─────────────────────────────────┘
```

I hate toolbars. Despise them. But that doesn't stop Microsoft from making them, so I'm learning to deal with them. If for some reason you decide that you'd like a toolbar in your own program, you could figure out how to code it all from scratch. Or you could use Toolbar Manager.

Toolbar Manager provides an API for creating toolbars. You can choose the size (small icons or large icons), and you can even have a "sliding" toolbar with a mini-scroll-thing at the bottom, as Figure 7-1 shows.

Quick, call the user-interface police! I think Narayan got carried away while coding this. If the point of a toolbar is to show you all of your options, and to make them readily available, then why hide them? The scroll-thingy should have been smothered at birth.

But if you just want to make normal toolbars, give this a try. The API is a bit convoluted, but decipherable. It handles things like off-screen pixmaps, floating windows, and palette window definitions, all of which generally give me hives.

If your program is public domain or freeware, Toolbar manager is free. If you are making shareware, the cost is the equivalent of three copies of your shareware product. Either

Figure 7-1. *This sample toolbar from Toolbar Manager can make your programs easier to use. Uh-huh*

way, you must put a notice in your "About" box that gives appropriate credit to SNR.

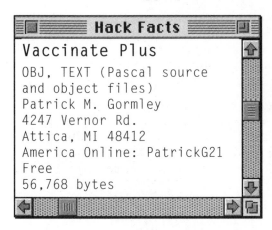

```
███ ██ ███ Hack Facts ███ ██
Vaccinate Plus                    ▲

OBJ, TEXT (Pascal source
and object files)
Patrick M. Gormley
4247 Vernor Rd.
Attica, MI 48412
America Online: PatrickG21
Free                              ▼
56,768 bytes
◄  ▓▓                         ►  ▣
```

Viruses are coming! Viruses are coming! Michelangelo will wipe your hard drive! Call Dan Rather! Alert the President! Granny, get the guns!

It wasn't too long ago that the great fourth estate, our beloved press, went ga-ga over a virus called Michaelangelo. It was supposed to erase your hard drive on April Fools' Day. Lucky for us Mac users, it was restricted to the DOS world, but the resultant hype and absolutely frantic predictions went unrestricted. Peter Jennings told people on the six o'clock news to back up their hard drive, nagging like he was their mother or something. Like I'm going to do *anything* that Peter Jennings tells me to. And what happened? Not much. A few people got their hard drives wiped out—I guess they lived in caves or something.

Ever since, the viral menace has been out of the news. And since System 7 came out for the Mac, viruses have been relatively unheard of. Have viruses run their course? I doubt it. More likely the guys who wrote viruses graduated from high school and had to get real jobs.

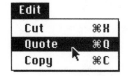

```
Edit
Cut       ⌘H
Quote     ⌘Q
Copy    ▶ ⌘C
```

It turns out to be very difficult to devise a theory to describe the universe all in one go.
—Stephen Hawking

Even so, it's quite possible that some 12-year-old kid, after breaking her leg on her skateboard and being stuck in a hospital bed for two weeks, could whip up some nasty little virus on her PowerBook to keep her brain from imploding out of sheer boredom. Were this to happen, would your programs be ready?

If your answer is no, look to Vaccinate Plus. This simple code object, which you link into your program using either C or Pascal, checks the size of all your resources. If it notices a change in the size, it returns an error. It's up to your code to report the error to the user. (Might I suggest a nice modal dialog box?)

Many commercial programs already do this. I was pleasantly surprised by ClarisWorks one day, when it told me it had been infected by "Scores" and needed to be replaced. It's good to do this for your users, and it doesn't cost you anything in terms of code: just link in Vaccinate Plus.

You will need to have your resources finalized before you can use Vaccinate Plus, so save it for the last bit of coding. The author suggests setting compiler variables, so the virus checking code isn't run until after you're done making changes to the program. Here's the sample code he provides:

```
{$IFC DEVELOPMENT}
{$ELSEC}
if not (ApplicationCanRun) then begin
    {Any necessary clean-up code}
    Halt;
end;
{$ENDC}
```

Set "DEVELOPMENT" to TRUE while working on the code, and FALSE when making an application build. The routine ApplicationCanRun is provided by Vaccinate Plus. It does all the dirty work, and simply returns a TRUE or FALSE. Cool!

Note

This won't protect your software against all viruses at all times. It simply checks for conditions where extra resources have been added to the program, or resources have gotten larger. This is not total protection; it is conceivable that a future virus might not work this way. Or, a virus that knew how Vaccinate Plus works could fool it; because the author provides some source code, it wouldn't be difficult for someone to write such a virus. But using Vaccinate Plus is much better than not adding any protection to your program.

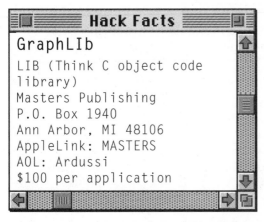

Hack Facts

GraphLIb

```
LIB (Think C object code
library)
Masters Publishing
P.O. Box 1940
Ann Arbor, MI 48106
AppleLink: MASTERS
AOL: Ardussi
$100 per application
```

Making graphs—those bar-chart things that Excel excels at—is always a tedious chore. But GraphLib makes it easy. And GraphLib comes in both C and Pascal flavors, so both sides of that holy war can benefit.

Here's how it works: first, you set up all the data structures. These are things like the name of the graph, the names of the axes, the scales of the axes, and so on. Then you decide what kind of graph you want it to be. Then you add points to the graph. Then you plot it. The routines exist in the precompiled code library file.

It's pretty simple, although you need to do a few things on your side first: you will probably plot the graph into an off-screen GrafPort so you can capture it to a PICT. So you'll need to create the port and do any associated housekeeping.

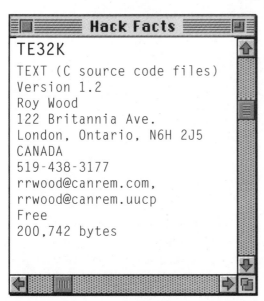

Hack Facts

TE32K

```
TEXT (C source code files)
Version 1.2
Roy Wood
122 Britannia Ave.
London, Ontario, N6H 2J5
CANADA
519-438-3177
rrwood@canrem.com,
rrwood@canrem.uucp
Free
200,742 bytes
```

When you write a Mac program that includes some editable text, most products use the TextEdit package built into the Mac ROMs. At least most non-word processors do: TeachText, AppleLink and America Online, to name just a few.

We do it because it's easy: just a few calls to the Mac toolbox, and voilà, instant editable text in a box. No sweating over the details. No problems. Except there's a limitation: the built-in TextEdit routines have a limit of 32K of data. And worse, they have a limit on the height of all the text, which must be less than 32k pixels tall.

TE32K solves this by providing a code library that you can use in place of the normal TextEdit routines. TE32K deals with the low-level drudgery of tracking all that text. It uses routine names and data structures that are almost exactly the same as the

standard TextEdit routines, so adding it to an existing program would be as easy as cake. Your program's calls would stay basically the same.

As TE32K author Roy Wood says, "There are a few other differences as well, most of which are shortcomings due to laziness on my part." At least he's honest. There are some odd redraw flashes in the text, but nothing serious, and since it comes with source code, you can fix the problems yourself if you have the inclination. As Wood says much better than I ever could, "Please feel free to modify it in whatever twisted way your warped little heart desires." Yeah.

this

is source code; you'll need to add the code to your project and compile it yourself. It's not object-oriented code, but if that's what you need, the author suggests using Chris Wysoki's CText. I think you could slip these routines into a descendent of the standard TCL CEditText class without much trouble, though. What's TCL, you ask? Read on.

Battle of the Sprites

I'm going to spend a significant amount of time discussing sprites because, IMHO, there aren't enough cool Mac games out there. One reason for this is that, despite the incredible power of QuickDraw, writing super-fast graphics routines isn't easy.

Every programmer who plays Andrew Welch's Maelstrom gets really excited about making Mac games. Some people even crank up the C compiler and get about two hours into writing a game, when they find themselves all mucked up in GWorlds and color pixmaps, at which point they start mumbling to themselves and singing little happy songs about color depths, then forget what the game they wanted to make was all about, so they just doodle some color icons in ResEdit before finally admitting defeat and returning to playing Maelstrom.

Using the right tools—which I'll cover in detail later in this chapter—you can concentrate on the game, and not worry about the mechanics behind the scenes. Who wants to worry about allocating pixmaps in MultiFinder temporary memory? Let someone else worry about that. You should spend your energy inventing the next Pac-Mac for Generation Z to waste their brain cells over.

About

Sprite (sprĭt) n. a graphical image, usually composed of several frames, capable of being moved around the screen. Generally, sprites handle the tough work of graphics programming for you: collision detection, multi-layering, and frame animation should be built into whatever package you're using.

Hack Facts

SpriteWorld
LIB (Think C object code library)
Version 1.0b3
Tony Myles
America Online: Suiryu
CompuServe: 72070,3000
Internet: suiryu@aol.com
Free
1,015,174 bytes (library, headers, and examples)

Tony Myles's SpriteWorld offers a truly complete sprite-management package. It has full, very readable documentation; a good API (application programming interface, or the routines you call to use it); and some very cool examples that are worth showing off to friends.

SpriteWorld provides routines that perform smooth multi-layered animation, with collision detection. SpriteWorld uses "custom bit-blitting routines" for drawing off-screen pixmaps—and for copying those pixmaps to the screen. It will synchronize the animation on millisecond intervals (thanks to the Time Manager). Figure 7-2 shows an example from SpriteWorld that illustrates how sprites exist in separate layers.

SpriteWorld's interfaces are simple to pick up. They follow the Macintosh ROM conventions: initialize a package, use the routines, clean up after yourself when you quit. It's pretty straightforward.

Figure 7-2. *The text is sandwiched between the two spinning globes*

You can import sprites from PICT resources, or from color icons. Color icons are better because they come with a mask for erasing the background; plus, you can edit them in ResEdit directly.

This package is popular. From what I hear on the net, many people are using this in shareware, and even in commercial software. The routines are certainly fast enough for any arcade-style games.

The latest version adds compatibility with non-QuickDraw machines, faster 8-bit animation, and minor bug fixes. The cost is nearly free; if you make any cool games with SpriteWorld, you must make Tony Myles a registered user and send him a copy. What a deal!

Join or die

I know it must seem like I have this holy vendetta against C, and well, I do. C sucks. To put it mildly.

I have wasted literally days at a time staring at C code, trying to figure out why something didn't compile, cursing the criminally vague Symantec C error messages, always wondering in the back of my mind if I had the time to convert everything to Pascal.

Sure, C is a very low-level language. You can do all kinds of tweaks to the code to improve performance. But these are the very tweaks that make C so unreadable. You know how I usually solve C syntax errors? Trial and error. I literally try one thing after another and recompile until the blasted thing works.

Years ago, pretty much everyone concurred on how horrible C was. Columns in Byte magazine used to decry its advent. But like the Blob overtaking that small town, C moved in and took over so slowly no one noticed. Now it's like those American Revolutionary War flags: "Join or Die." I feel besieged.

Symantec hasn't released an update to Think Pascal in eons, in the hope that Pascal programmers will just switch to C. I reported a Pascal bug to them almost two years ago:

if you run a QuickTime movie in the environment, when you quit the program, your machine will always crash. Always. Never fails. I reported it. Tech support verified it. I still have the fax. But they've never fixed it. And now they don't even pretend they're going to fix it. Code Warrior, a new environment from Metrowerks that offers both C and Pascal compilers, should offer some serious competition. Maybe Symantec will get on the ball and support their product.

Even with the minor bugs, Pascal trounces C in the leveraged-tools department. Why waste time tweaking your code? Before long we'll all be using RISC machines. All code will be screamingly fast, no matter how poorly written. We'll have cycles to burn. All that low-level C coding, all that byte-tweaking for speed--which is poor programming practice and will probably lead to a crash if you port that code to RISC--will have been pointless for the great majority of programmers.

Don't get me wrong. I program in C when my job requires it. But I don't like it. And only programmers who need low-level control of their machines will be using it in the future. To misquote those wonderful American Revolutionary flags, "Join and die."

```
═══ Hack Facts ═══

SAT

OBJ (Think Pascal code
library), PROJ (Think C
project)
Version 2.0b5
Ingemar Ragnemalm
Plöjaregatan 73
S-58330 Linköping
SWEDEN
ingemar@isy.liu.se
Free
991,620 bytes
```

Like SpriteWorld, SAT provides routines for animating sprites. But unlike the C-only SpriteWorld, SAT is provided as a code library for Pascal programmers (although there are C interface files, too).

SAT offers a few features that SpriteWorld doesn't:

- SAT works at any bit depth, and it detects switches on the fly. So if the user switches from 16 colors to 256 colors while playing your game, everything just keeps working. And if SAT can't use its high-speed bit-blitting routines, then it uses the Mac's built-in QuickDraw as a backup. SpriteWorld only works at 256 colors, so games that use it can't run on the Mac Plus, SE, or Classic.

- SAT provides routines to play sounds asynchronously (which means, the sound plays while you do other things, as opposed to HyperCard's freeze-the-Mac-while-playing-the-sound synchronous method). While this isn't terribly difficult to do yourself, it's nice that SAT handles it, so beginning programmers don't feel overwhelmed.

On the other hand, SpriteWorld does come with full source code. If you want to modify it or fix a bug that you've discovered, just open the code and edit away. SAT, on the other hand, is a compiled code object. There's no way to crawl inside and modify it.

SAT makes it easy to create sprite-based action games in Pascal, as Figure 7-3 shows. SAT handles the layering of sprites—as well as collision detection—automatically.

Figure 7-3. *With SAT you can easily produce sprite-based games in Pascal*

SAT uses resources of type *cicn* (color icons) to make its sprites. SpriteWorld can use cicns or PICTs. SpriteWorld sprites can be any size; SAT sprites must be in even multiples of 8 pixels wide. So there are trade-offs with both products.

According to the author, Ingemar Ragnemalm, SAT has been used by several popular Mac games, among them Bachman and Slime Invaders (both of which Ingemar wrote). Bachman is one of my favorites, too, so I was psyched to learn this. It's been tested in the real world, and we know it works.

SAT costs you nothing; however, you must send author Ingemar Ragnemalm a copy of whatever shareware or freeware you create with his SAT routines. If you want to use SAT in commercial software, contact Ingemar Ragnemalm first for licensing information.

Thinking Objectively: TCL Classes

When the Think Class Library, better known as TCL, debuted, it ushered in a whole new method of programming previously limited to users of such oddities as Smalltalk. The whole idea of a library of class, which was totally extensible via classes that could be shared with others, was new to most Mac programmers.

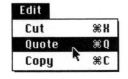

Make the enemy live up to their own book of rules.
—*Saul D. Alinsky,*
Rules for Radicals

Right after TCL came out, I took it for a test drive, matching it against a program I had been working on for about a month. In one week I had duplicated all of the work to date in TCL. That convinced me totally: OOP was not just a cool, hip buzzword, but was actually useful. I tossed out a month's worth of work—depressingly little had been done, to be honest—and never looked back.

(Not long after that, the owner of the company that enslaved me read something about Apple's application framework MacApp, and after much heated debate he made us switch to it. MacApp is wonderful but much more complex than TCL. We threw out months of work—again—and started over in MacApp. My company never did finish that product. Hey, all the cool programming tools in the world won't save you from stupid management.)

The best place to look for TCL classes is on the net. Keep an ear to the ground and watch the network traffic in the comp.sys.mac.oop.tcl and comp.sys.mac.programmer newsgroups. The FTP site ftp.brown.edu serves as the net repository for TCL classes (although this may change soon). This is also where you can find the TCL FAQ (Frequently Asked Questions list), notes on bugs in the TCL classes, and the entire comp.sys.mac.oop.tcl newsgroup archive, which is searchable by WAIS (Wide Area Information Search).

Here's a list of all of the classes available on the ftp.brown.edu server as of press time. You can find these in the directory pub/tcl/classes.

CCoolAbout-1.0b3-P-classes

CCoolDecorator-1.0b2-P-classes

CDateText-1.0-C-classes

CDecimalText-1.0-C++-classes

CDeviceIter-1.0.1-C++-classes

CDictionary-1.0-C-classes

CDividedPane-1.0-C-classes

CDragAcrossTable-1.0b1-C-classes

CFile-1.1-C-classes

CFlexiDataFile-1.1-C-classes

CHiliteDialog_CStringArray-1.0-C-classes

CIconBuddy-1.0-C-classes

CIconFamily-1.0-C-classes

CJanitor-1.0-C++-classes

CListMgrPane-1.0-C-classes

CMIDI-2.2-C-classes

CMovie_Run-1.0-C-classes

CMultStdPopupPane-1.0-C-classes

CMultStdPopupPane-2.0-C++-classes

COrderedList-2-C-classes

CPEditText-1.2-C-classes

CPasswordText-1.0-C-classes

CPixelWorld-1.2-C-classes

CPrefFile-1.0-C-classes

CPrefsFile-1.2b2-P-classes

CRandom-1.0-C-classes

CSICNPane-1.0-C-classes

CScrollList-1.0-C-classes

CScrollorama-1.1-C-classes

CStaticTextPane-1.0-C-classes

CStatusBar-1.0-C-classes

CStatusPane-1.0-C++-classes

CStream-1.0-C-classes

CTCP-1.0-C-classes

CTerminalPane-1.0-C-classes

CTextFile-1.1-P-classes

CThermometerDirector-1.0-C-classes

CTreeViewer-1.0-C-classes

CVblSync-1.0.1-C-classes

CWhoisEngine-1.0-C-classes

CWindowZoomer-1.0b3-P-classes

CXCharGrid-1.0-C-classes

CommunicationsToolbox-1.0-C-classes

Intelligent_Classes-1.0-C-classes

ItemClass-1.0-C-classes

MacTCP-1.2-C-classes

NodeViewer-1.0-C-classes

TCLscript-1.0d1-C++-classes

TurboTCP-1.0.1-C-classes

7

Allow me to recommend a few favorites:

- **CPrefsFile** This class works under both System 6 and System 7, and implements the standard behavior for a preferences file, (i.e. it lives in a folder called "Preferences" inside the System folder).

- **CMovieRun** Opens and displays a QuickTime movie in a TCL pane.

- **CMIDI** Written by the good Paul Ferguson, CMIDI provides a nifty class for communicating with MIDI-compatible musical instruments.

Coming Up Next:
From Theory to Reality

Writing a program is a lot like inventing a hypothesis. It's all well and good in the lab, but until you test it in the real world, it means nothing. That's where debugging comes in. The real world is a cruel and harsh place. Doubtless, your programs will crash countless times before you can perfect them. Don't take it personally. Everyone writes crashers.

The next chapter will show off some cool debugging tools that make the tracking down and elimination of bugs in your code as easy and painless as possible. Lace up them combat boots, flick off the safeties—we're heading into the hottest LZ yet. Destination: Macsbug.

The Zen of Good Code: Debuggers

When an airplane crashes, after all the survivors are rescued, but before the casualties are sent home and the luggage is scanned for valuables, there is usually a prime objective: find the black box.

The black box, the flight recorder, is the treasure sought by all the investigators. Within the confines of that little box lie the secrets of the disaster. Inside that box is nothing other than Just What the Hell Happened.

Computers crash, too, though far less dramatically; but your Mac didn't really come with anything like a black box. It would be great if a dialog box popped up to tell you that your hard drive had iced over or wind shear on your keyboard made Word 5.1 seize up your Centris. Luckily, our hacker pals are out there, putting together virtual black boxes for your Mac that tell you exactly what happened, and how you can recover and get on with your life, armed with new knowledge so that this won't happen again.

Computers are useless. They can only give you answers.

—Pablo Picasso

In the computer world, these black boxes are called debuggers.

Slinking Inside the Heart of the Machine

So your program crashes. What now? Debuggers are the only way to find out what's happening deep inside the bowels of your computer. This chapter will cover the basics of using Apple's popular Macsbug debugger with some handy external commands you can get for free. Plus we'll talk about the ABZMon debugger, which is public domain and widely available.

Freely available shareware programmer's helpers abound. In addition to the expensive stuff, we'll concentrate on the free stuff that can put more jolt into your programming sessions than your cola.

The Big Picture: Memory

The best debugging tools, besides actual debuggers, fall into that class of program that shows you information about memory allocation. After all, your program is nothing more than bits in memory. And probably three out of four crashes are caused by accessing memory locations that you shouldn't.

Back in Chapter 4 I talked about a program called ZoneRanger. I like it quite a bit, but many people on the net have pointed to Swatch as their favorite memory watcher. And, to be honest, I use Swatch more than ZoneRanger, but only because Swatch is simpler to use.

Hack Facts

Swatch
APPL
Version 1.2.2
Joe Holt
Internet: jholt@adobe.com
America Online: Jholt
AppleLink: ADOBE.APDENG
(attn: joe)
415-962-2097 (voice)
41,076 bytes

Swatch, short for system watch, displays a graph of the memory usage of all applications. You can zoom in on a graph for more detail using the magnifying glass tool.

Swatch displays the heap in an easy-to-grok color display, as shown in Figure 8-1. By clicking on the application's name, you will compact that application's heap. Why would you want to do that? Well, compacting the

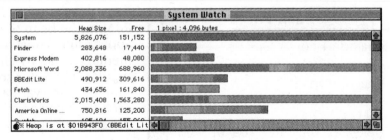

Figure 8-1. *Heaps shown in Swatch's color display. [Clicking on the bomb icon, shown in the lower-left corner of the screen, drops you into the debugger]*

heap generally involves moving memory blocks around, And the system may compact the heap at any time, usually when you least expect it. When the system does that, poorly written code of yours may crash.

I use Swatch's free memory display to find memory leaks. Try this: run an application you've made, and then run Swatch. Jot down the amount of free memory your application has. Now open and close a few windows. Eventually, return all the windows to the state they were in when you opened the application and check Swatch again. Now jot down this number, too.

Do the numbers match? If not, you probably have a leak. By carefully checking the numbers, you can determine how much you lose each time you open a window. That may help you find the data structure that's not being deallocated.

There is a DCMD (a debugger command—see the "Adding to Macsbug" section at the end of this chapter for details) for Macsbug called Leaks, but it can't handle big OOPs programs that allocate lots of handles; there's just too much going on for it to track. In that case, Swatch is not a bad choice. But then, Ramadillo (reviewed next) can help you find leaks, too.

```
Hack Facts

Ramadillo
APPL
Russ Coffman
Aldus Corp., Persuasion Div.
Dallas, TX
Internet: Armadillo@AOL.com
America Online: AFC Russ
AppleLink: BSTOUT
Sort of free (see below)
23,119 bytes
```

Ramadillo graphically displays the free RAM in the heap of one other open application. Ramadillo helps you discover memory leaks by checking memory at regular intervals (you set the amount of time per interval), and at the end of each time period it shows you the difference between memory snapshots.

Ramadillo's graph isn't quite as cute or informative as Swatch's graph, but it's much better suited to the task of finding memory leaks because it gives the deltas you'd normally have to compute by hand, as Figure 8-2 shows.

Adobe vs. Aldus

How about that fierce rivalry between Adobe and Aldus? They make competing illustration programs, and now competing shareware heap-watching programs. Like two superpowers fueling the space program, their battle enables all of us third-world denizens to benefit. (Just look what we got from the space program: Tang, ballpoint pens that write upside down, and freeze-dried ice cream.)

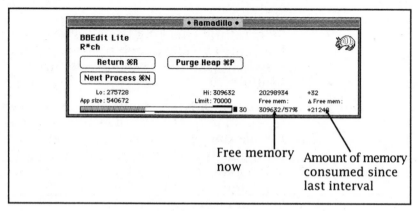

Figure 8-2. *Ramadillo shows the deltas in memory use between heap snapshots*

Ramadillo is listed as "Persuasionware." To quote Russ Coffman: "Ramadillo is Altering Reality: Utilities for a Better Life Persuasionware. If you need a presentation program, please look at Aldus Persuasion and help me keep my job! It's No. 1 anyway, but every little bit helps." Ya dig? Help the man out.

Notes from the trenches—don't double dispose

A few days ago, I had an interesting crash that took a while to figure out. I had a handle that held a Mac sound. The second time a sound finished playing, my program would crash. (Well, there's actually more to it than that, but for the sake of brevity let's stick with this explanation.)

It turns out I was disposing the sound handle twice. This really screws up the Memory Manager; the second time through, it does all sorts of awful things (like screwing up the master pointer list).

Apple has released a couple of extensions on its Developer CD-ROMs: DoubleTrouble and DisposeResource. DoubleTrouble will detect this situation (that is, when you dispose of a handle twice). DisposeResource will alert you to a similar condition: when you call DisposeHandle on a resource handle (which is also a big no-no).

Also, you can get the infamous EvenBetterBusError, which detects the dangerous usage of nil handles. I used to run my system with EvenBetterBusError on all the time, but it depressed me to see how many commercial applications actually read and write to nil handles. Now I only run it when I am testing my own apps. All three are available on the Apple Developer CD-ROMs, or on Apple's ftp site (ftp.apple.com).

8

```
═══════════ Hack Facts ═══════════

Programmer's Key
Version 1.4.2
Paul Mercer
P.O. Box 160165
Cupertino, CA 95014-0165
Internet: pmercer@apple.com
AppleLink: MERCER1
Free
6,510 bytes
```

It used to be that every Mac had hard-wired switches for interrupt and reset. Sometimes you had to put the switches on yourself, but all machines had them. And programmers would often use both switches.

In more recent Macs, these switches have disappeared. So what's a programmer to use in their place? Programmer's Key solves this dilemma. It substitutes the POWER key for the interrupt and reset switches, since almost anyone who wants to use those switches has a keyboard with a POWER key. This extension will drop into the debugger—the functional equivalent of hitting the interrupt switch—when you press the COMMAND-POWER key. (On PowerBooks, press COMMAND-DELETE.)

Tip

Hold the OPTION key down and you'll drop into the debugger in the frontmost process only.

```
═══════════ Hack Facts ═══════════

Debug Window
APPL
Version 2.0
Ken Ledbetter
America Online: Kledbetter
63,505 bytes
Free
```

Half the time when you're debugging, you're chasing your own tail. For instance, let's say you have this huge array of names, and for the sake of argument, you've written a routine that will print them all on command, so you can see if they're entered in memory correctly.

So you run the program and bring up the names. Whoops! Garbage fills the window. What happened? You can't be certain. Is the problem in the array, or the code that displays it?

Heisenberg was right with his uncertainty principle (he said that just by looking at something you change it), but fortunately we've got DebugWindow (unlike our particle-physics colleagues, who have nothing of the sort).

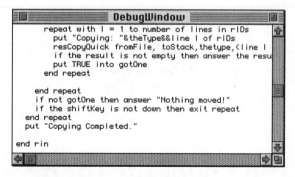

Figure 8-3. *DebugWindow will display any text you ask it to, as well as hexadecimal values*

DebugWindow is a separate application that runs by itself. This means you can be confident that your code can't contaminate it, and that it can't contaminate your code.

The author, Ken Ledbetter, provides a few C routines and HyperCard XCMDs to let you print stuff to the window. You can print text or hexadecimal numbers. I typed in HyperCard "xDebug the script of this stack" to get the display shown in Figure 8-3. You can even have your lines of text time-stamped.

While this isn't extraordinarily helpful in HyperCard—where the "answer" command takes care of displaying variables for you—it can be a godsend when working with C programs, or long values in HyperCard.

Too bad Ken Ledbetter didn't include a Pascal library. Since he's using AppleEvents to send the text back and forth, it probably would be a simple matter to create the analogous Pascal routines. I'll leave this as an exercise to the reader.

The canonical (if I were playing Scrabble, I'd challenge you on *canonical,* which means authoritative, official, or orthodox) set of Macintosh system error codes is spread across six volumes of *Inside Macintosh* (and on countless interface files). And who can remember that system error 87 is "couldn't find WDEF?" Not me, that's for sure. So I like to use an online reference. And the best online reference I've found is System Errors.

System Errors is an application that displays the list of error codes on several pages. You can scroll through the text or jump to any page. Explanations never exceed one line, so sometimes they're a bit cryptic, but you can usually figure out what the message means with little trouble.

The Low End Theory: Debuggers

While those high-level heap displayers will show you all kinds of valuable information, they can't do it all. Sometimes you've just gotta hunker down and crawl inside that code at the lowest level to figure out what the hell's going on. And to do that, you need a debugger.

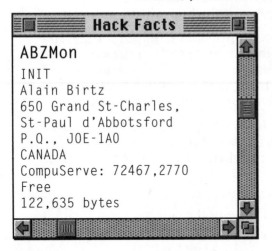

Although Apple will sell you their debugger Macsbug—and others will sell you TMON and MacNosy, worthy competition to Macsbug—only one person will give you a debugger with full documentation for free. Alain Birtz.

ABZMon is a debugger, like Macsbug. It loads as an init and is immediately ready—you can even use it to debug other inits. You can drop into it by using any of these methods (which are the same ones you use to drop into Macsbug):

- Using the interrupt switch or Programmer's Key

- Using the "Debugger" call

- Using the "DebugStr" call, with a Pascal string

- Using the "DebugNum" call, which is unique to ABZMon

Once you land in the debugger, you'll notice that it looks nothing like Macsbug, but elements are still vaguely familiar. The difference is because ABZMon uses homegrown versions of the Macintosh's windows and menus to display its information. (It can't use the real things, or else it would depend on certain ROM calls that may have crashed already.) What's familiar are window contents: displays of registers, a memory dump, and code disassembly.

the The scrolling windows in particular are very powerful. If you see an address, you can double-click to see its contents. You can zip through a memory dump in no time using the pseudo-scroll bars. And if you want to, you can even display a text file from your hard drive (a lifesaver if you need to compare source code with the debugger code).

If a Mac crashes in a forest, does a programmer somewhere writhe in agony?

What is the sound of one hand clapping? What happens when an irresistible force meets an immovable object? Can God make a stone so large that even He cannot lift it? How does one find bugs in a debugger? These are the great philosophical questions of our time.

8

I have to admit, I didn't have the guts to do more than just run this on my Mac and look at the windows. When it came to actual debugging, my knees got weak. Debugging a debugger? That takes bigger *cojones* than I can muster. So I had a friend well-versed in assembly language give it a whirl. (Remember, I'm Mister High-Level Language. Assembly gives me hives.)

My main man, programmer Kevin Martin (let's give him a hand), said that ABZMon worked very well. He especially liked the windows for the disassembly listings. It's easy to see why, as anyone who has tried digging through code knows the pain of a thousand keystrokes. (As they say, even the pain of a thousand keystrokes begins with a single crash.)

Our tendency to concentrate power in the hands of a few men deeply concerns me.
—Barry Goldwater

The whole idea of a freeware debugger is a little strange at first, but once you get used to it, it's cool. It has features that no one else has really emulated: the ability to take screendumps, for instance, or read text files while debugging.

I'm sure there will be many more features added. I recommend that everyone try ABZMon for a little while, just to see what it's like. After all, it won't cost you anything except your time. But then, time is money, so maybe...oh, never mind.

Kill your Macintosh

So it's three A.M., you've just crashed into the debugger for the septillionth time, there's absolutely no reason why your code should crash, you've banged your head against the proverbial wall so many times your forehead is forming a flat spot. What to do? Shoot your Mac. Since this book is about tools for programmers, I'd be remiss if I didn't recommend the best guns around for blowing your Mac away.

Now let me point out that I don't recommend this. Guns are dangerous. They're not toys. And Macs are expensive non-toys too, unless you can get a good deal on a cheap government surplus Mac Plus. (By the way, don't keep your gun near your Mac. Debugging late at night can make you want to play Russian roulette, and with today's semiautomatic handguns, it would be a game sorely lacking in suspense.)

The Beretta 92F is a 9-mm handgun with a muzzle velocity above the speed of sound. It packs a helluva whallop when its slug hits a CRT. The Glock 10-mm is a nice choice, too, except that it doesn't have a real safety.

Shotgun. Any brand will do, but I'm partial to a Mossberg 12-gauge. This will make your Mac look like it went through Desert Storm on the wrong side of the border. Serious case damage will be a very popular look on campus this fall. Use bird shot or rock salt if you're more interested in the cosmetic effect than actually destroying your Mac (poseur!).

If you can't afford the high cost of a first-class handgun, the shareware equivalent of this programmer's tool would be a large rock, steel-toed boots, a crowbar, aluminum bat (unplug the Mac first), or golf club.

Make sure you use some kind of hollow-point ammo (the FBI rates Hydra-Shock as the best brand), else you're liable to put the bullet through the Mac and into your coworker in the next cubicle. Aim for the center of the screen. If you cover it with clear adhesive tape first, it will make a really cool spider's web pattern that the implosion won't wreck. Remember, depending on the model Mac you're aiming at, shooting the monitor isn't necessarily the same thing as shooting the Mac itself. Don't lose sight of this elusive technicality in the heat of the moment. Shoot to kill--at least two slugs through the motherboard, then drop the gun to your side and walk away quickly. Don't run, and don't look anyone directly in the eye, but don't avoid anyone's gaze either.

And remember, there's no shame in shooting your Mac. We all want to do it. Hell, if Elvis had been a hacker, there's no doubt he would have shot his SE/30.

This sidebar is dedicated to Ruffin Prevost and David Ramsey, who should both know why.

Gambling is not as destructive as war or boring as pornography. It is not as immoral as business or as suicidal as watching television. And the percentages are better than religion.
—Mario Puzo

Adding to Macsbug

The standard debugger, of course, is Apple's own Macsbug. It's based on an earlier Motorola debugger product—believe it or not, the "Macs" in the name has nothing to do with Macintoshes! Pointless trivia aside, all serious programmers must have and use Macsbug to struggle through the last and bloodiest stage of development: debugging.

While Macsbug technically isn't shareware, it's about as ubiquitous as the most popular freeware programs around. If you don't have Macsbug, you can buy a copy from APDA, or if you're a developer, you're likely to find the latest

8

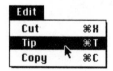

For information on writing your own DCMDs, refer to the Apple publication Debugging Macintosh Software with Macsbug.

version of it on a developer's CD lying around your shop somewhere.

Earlier in this book I've given some Macsbug tips. Those tips dealt with the commands that were built into Macsbug. But what if Macsbug is lacking commands you need?

That's right, you guessed it: Macsbug can take external commands, just like HyperCard. They're called DCMDs (for Debugger Commands), and they are just code fragments that Macsbug calls upon. You install them by copying the "dcmd" resource into your "Debugger Prefs" file in your System Folder.

some

of these DCMDs have been in my system for ages, and their origins are lost in the mists of time. I've included whatever contact information I could locate. In general, you can find these DCMDs on AppleLink, info-mac, or on America Online.

If you're not a programmer, then much of this list will be meaningless to you. Sorry 'bout that, but then, if you're not a Mac programmer, why are you reading this book?

DCMD COMMAND	DESCRIPTION
AEDesc	Prints out contents of an Apple event Descriptor.
AEDescData	Prints out contents of an Apple event Descriptor from imbedded descriptor.
aevt	Prints out contents of an Apple event with parameters formatted.
cards (v1.0b1)	Displays information about cards installed in your machine.
codecseq	Displays codec sequences.
dizy	Installs and uninstalls the discipline package, which checks every call you make to the Mac ROMs to assure you're not doing anything stupid.

DCMD COMMAND	DESCRIPTION
DPRAM	Displays value of parameter RAM. You must know the address you want to view.
drive [drvNum|dRefNum]	Displays drive queue information for the given drive number, driver number, or all drives.
drvr [refnum|num]	Displays driver information for the given refnum or all installed drivers.
echo	Echoes the command line parameters
error [expr]	Displays text message corresponding to error number in expr. Handy for looking up those weird error messages.
events	Keeps track of a user-selectable number of the most recent events in the event queue. You can then view this list.
file [fRefNum|"file name"]	Displays file information for the given fRefNum, file name or all open files.
heap	Displays information about all the existing heap blocks.
leaks	Watches the stack crawl to track down potential memory leaks in your code.
menu	Displays information about the currently installed menus.
printf "format" arg	Just like the C printf, except its output goes to the debugger. Very handy for C freaks.
proc (1.0a1)	Lists all processes running under MultiFinder.
RAMDump (1.1b1)	Dumps all memory to floppy disks.
RD [resType[resNum]] [,"fileName"|fileNum]	Displays the specified resources and resource files. Very handy for tracking down resource-file-chain problems.
SD (1.0a1)	In theory, this lists the elements in the shutdown queue. I've never gotten it to work, however; it always reports that the Shutdown Manager is patched out. Your mileage may vary.
SPRAM	Assigns a value to parameter RAM. You must know the address you want to set.

8

DCMD COMMAND	DESCRIPTION
ssc [addr]	Displays the stack frame chain starting at addr (default is ra6).
stopif	Stops in Macsbug if expr is true. Otherwise continues execution of the command line.
stopxpp	Causes all XPP sessions to time out soon.
sysswell <buffer size>	Installs or removes a buffer in the System heap of specifed size.
systop	Installs and locks a four-byte handle at the top of the system heap; the handle is not installed.
thing ["thing type"]	Displays thing information for the given thing type or all known things. Things are used by the Component Manager.
timebase	"Everything you never wanted to know about timebases." Timebases are used by QuickTime data structures.
timedump	Displays info about active time mgr tasks and time mgr globals.
USFN [Address of userFnHead from VMG]	Displays the number of user functions currently queued up.
vbl	Displays vertical retrace queue information.
VMDump	Displays status of pages of memory.
vol	Displays volume information for a given vrefnum, volume name, or all mounted volumes.
where	Displays information about an address or trap. If no parameter exists, it displays the PC.
whip	Finds the name and addr of a linked patch.

*The first law of war
is to preserve
ourselves and
destroy the enemy.*
— *Mao Tse-Tung*

The Art of Debugging

I can't teach you how to effectively use a debugger like Macsbug—that would take a whole book. In fact, Scott Knaster's classic *How To Write Macintosh Software* is just that book. If you need more tutorials on making the most of Macsbug, check it out. (You should be ashamed if you don't already have it.)

Even so, the shareware in this chapter should go a long way toward making your debugging sessions quicker, less hair-tearingly frustrating, and more successful.

With these tools, we've made it to the other side. Good work! Now you're ready to fight the code wars on your own. Take these supplies, head for the safety of your own Macintosh, and dig in. Sure, you've got a long, hard fight ahead of you. But you've got strength, stamina, and some great tools to help you.

Good luck!

8

011010 11000110 0011010 11001001 100010001

011010 11000110 0011010 11001001 100010001

0011010 11001001 100010001

part
3

The Extra Stuff

How to Make a Million Bucks in Shareware

Ha, ha. You can't make a million bucks in shareware. You can, however, make decent money in shareware if you follow a few simple rules. This appendix is a guide to writing software for money, without the hassle and bother of finding a software publisher.

It's the dream of every programmer. Start your own software company, compete with the big boys, break into the market, get treated to trade shows, a speaking spot at MacWorld, perhaps a review in *MacWeek*. Unfortunately, this dream rarely comes true. It costs huge sums of money to start a software company these days. From the incredible ad dollars it takes to crack the major publications, to the expensive yet imperative trade shows, a software company needs cash. The era of garage-based software companies is waning.

the good news is, if you release your creations as shareware, you're living the entrepreneurial life. You're your own boss. You write the programs you think need to be written. No idiot managers hang over your shoulders. You get direct feedback from your users, without marketing bozos interfering.

Plus, shareware gets lots of free credit the big boys can't buy. For example, Now Software can't get the free press coverage a shareware offering like BeHierarchical can. This is a huge advantage only shareware authors can enjoy.

While working on this book and others, I've talked to countless shareware authors. I've learned a few of their rules for success, and I've added my own observations. Although following the suggestions in this appendix doesn't guarantee great shareware, it can optimize whatever potential your shareware creation has.

When it comes to shareware, there is a Golden Rule. Price it seriously. *And* take it seriously.

For a while, there was a nasty trend of $3 shareware. Some tiny, insignificant program would be let loose on the world, and the author would beg for a couple of bucks in the About dialog box.

Forget it, folks. No one takes this seriously, least of all you. You probably can't afford to support a program that makes you $15 a week. And no one wants to pay for unsupported software. If you write a small program that doesn't do much, and you haven't fully tested it, don't make it shareware. Release it as freeware, or postcardware, or beerware, or whateverware. Just not shareware. When people pay money, they expect results. This is not to say that low-priced shareware is a bad idea. Larry Harris released his program FontFaker, at the bargain price of just $5. That's all he felt it was worth. But he fully supports and stands behind his software, and in return, he gets enough cash to splurge on a pizza every so often.

When chosing between two evils, I always like to try the one I've never tried before.

—Mae West

how much to charge? Once again, don't ask for too little. Be serious in your effort. Offer a good product, with good support, for a reasonable price. At the moment, $25 seems to be the average, although there has been successful shareware at both ends of the price curve ($5 for FontFaker, $40 for Mariner).

Bottom line: I'd recommend $25 for a good, general-purpose utility program. Stick to $25 for even a high-quality game. Exceed this amount at your own peril.

Readme the Right Way

Think of the readme file as a voodoo doll. It's the physical manifestation of you, the shareware author, in the hands of the user. You get to be cute, witty, knowledgeable, informative, and damn helpful.

But if you're not, your users will poke needles into your eyes. A bad readme with inaccurate information, poor instructions, or out-of-date version information can deaden otherwise glitzy shareware.

Here's a sample readme. Notice that it includes all sorts of important information. Feel free to rip off this sample. If you don't rip this off, make sure you include the same information in your readmes. (Note that this is not really complete; it's only an example.)

[Name] MacFizzBin

[Version number] 1.0b3

[Copyright notice] c 1994 Rob Terrell

[Contact information] AOL: RobTerrell
Internet: Robt@vnet.net

[Short description] This program leaps tall buildings in a single bound.

[Requirements] AppleScript, QuickTime 1.61

[Known incompatibilities] Incompatible with NowMenus

[Installation instructions] Double-click the installer program

---

[How to use] Double-click the application from the Finder. Nothing will happen

---

[Version History] 1.0b3 - Fixed bug under System 7.
1.0b2 - Corrected spelling in menus.
1.0b1 - First general release.

Don't be afraid to let your readme have a friendly, folksy air. People like to read things that have a personal touch. (Or so my editors keep telling me, chapter after tortuous chapter.) Just don't overdo it. Don't be overly cute. Get to the point—in style, with a little wit and flair—but don't get crazy on us.

Test Like the Wind

I actually released a shareware program recently. My beta testers are a good bunch, and are finding all kinds of stupid mistakes I made. Better them than real users, or heaven forbid, the editors at *MacWorld!*

Far too many shareware authors overlook the testing phase. I'm tired of readme files that say things like "this works on my Centris, but I've heard it may not work on a Performa." Get real, kids. Test it. Find someone online who can test it for you.

In chapter 3 there is a section "Passing the Test" on testing your software. Do it. Test on every class of machine, from the lowly 68000 to the latest PowerPC. Try different system software versions.

Call the Exterminator

Bug fixes are more important than new features. Get your existing user base working, bug free, before adding bells and whistles. Your reputation will be much better if folks don't crash.

I recently loaded a shareware program, double-clicked it, and immediately slammed my Mac into a virtual tree. Bad news. Somebody never tested their shareware, at least not on my kind of Mac.

Good users will start removing INITS and restarting to try and find the troublemaker. I'm not a good user. Hey, if my machine crashed when I ran shareware, the shareware must be at fault, right? I mean, the Mac was working just fine before. (This is the kind of thinking you're up against.)

If You Love Something, Set It Free

Once you've written the program, had it sufficiently tested, written the readme, and put the whole thing into a stuffit archive, you're ready to release it to the world. This can be a scary step. It also can be thrilling. It's exciting to see one of your creations online!

There are a few places you must be sure and upload your creation. Make sure you post it in the appropriate forum, and also send it to the forum leader for his or her consideration.

CompuServe
America Online
sumex-aim@stanford.edu
michigan archives

Also post it on GEnie, Delphi, AppleLink, and other eWorlds as you see fit. If you don't have access to any of these, check with friends, local computer stores, or user groups for folks who can post it for you.

Tip

Make sure people know about your program. Post notices that your program is available on all relevant message boards. Tell what it does and how much it costs. List any special features and any cool comments from your beta testers.

A Gentle Prodding vs. a Cattle Prod

You need to get paid. How do you ensure that users—who will acquire your shareware for free—actually end up paying you for it?

Shame them into it. File Buddy displays a dialog box reminding users to pay every three days. That seems like just the right amount of time; any more, and people get annoyed. Any less, and they forget all about paying you.

A

Tip

Don't piss off your users. Programs that cripple the
softwar—that is, deactivate features until the fee is
paid—have done very poorly historically.

Once users pay, they should be able to disable the
reminders. A good way to do this is to offer some way to
enter a registration code into the program, say, from the
About This Program dialog box.

Commercial software often uses a complex scheme of
verifying serial numbers to determine if the code is valid.
(This is usually done by XORing the serial number with a
large prime number and checking the result.) Making up a
special code for each user is more effort than the average
shareware author can afford. Instead, create some secret
code and have it work for all users. Odds are, people won't
share the code. And the determined few who really want to
crack your program will crack it no matter how sophisticated
your code. (Shame on anyone low enough to crack
shareware, for Christ's sake.)

Collecting the Loot

In the end, it may be that only a small percentage of your
users will actually pay you. Keep in mind that the easier you
make it for people to pay you, the more money you will
make. So make every effort to make it easy. Be sure your
address is clearly visible in both the readme and the About
box. Include an option to print a registration form; and offer
a fax-based registration service if you can.

CompuServe has a service called SWReg, which lets users
charge shareware fees to a credit card. This is the easiest way
for users to pay. Although CompuServe levies a 15-percent
surcharge, you'll make up that money in extra registrations. In
order for you to be successful, it's imperative that users be
able to register their software this way.

Tip
Don't forget that Uncle Sam wants his cut. The IRS will snag you if you're not careful. The money you get from users is, after all, income, and there's a whole raft of tax laws dealing with money from self-employment, which writing shareware is.

The Final 10 Percent

When you get lucky do you call that special friend the morning after? If you're not that kind of person, well, no wonder you're still single. If you want to be successful in shareware (and romance) respond. Answer your users' letters. Address the comments, both kind and unkind. Make it clear that you've heard them, and thank them for their input. That final 10 percent of the effort—which usually takes 90 percent of your time—is spent in support. Take the time to do it right.

if your callers/emailers/visitors (yikes!) haven't paid, urge them gently to do so. Remember, selling yourself and your wares is a necessary evil in this world. Your email to users will be the closest thing to a sales pitch you'll ever get (besides the actual shareware and readme). If you hate sales as much as I do, then practice the fine art of the soft sell. Don't be pushy; be a good, honest, and deserving human being. Good things will follow.

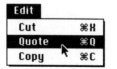

Keep up appearances, whatever you do.
  —Charles Dickens

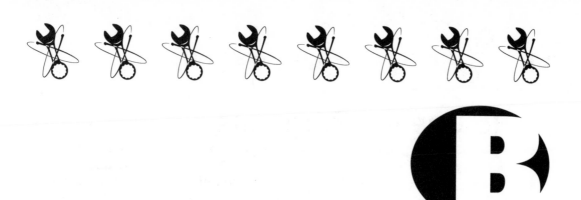

Try 'em Out for Size: Exploring the Disk

You'd think, for the incredibly low cost of this book, all you'd get would be the pages contained herein. I know I would. But no! There's more! We've taken a bunch of programs reviewed in this book and included them on a disk.

To Install the Programs

To install these programs, insert the floppy disk into your computer. Double-click the file "PROGRAMMER'S COOKBOOK INSTALLER.". After the splash screen, you will see some text explaining what's going on. Click the Continue button.

At this point, you will need to choose a location on your hard drive to which you can save the files. The entire set of files, when decompressed, takes up about 3 MB of disk space. After you click Okay, the files will be installed.

Note

Some anti-viral programs, such as Virex, GateKeeper, SAM, etc. may prevent the installer from working properly. If so, you may want to disable any anti-viral programs you have installed before performing the installation.

To Use the Programs

The next section lists the programs and gives you some simple instructions for using the shareware included on the disk. These instructions are not all-inclusive; please refer to the readme files that come with each program for complete instructions.

Also, remember this important point: pay for what you use. These authors worked long and hard to create these programs. If you use something, pay for it.

Note

Tech support for these programs is provided soley by the program's author. Please do not call me, the editors, or the pubisher of this book for tech support for any program contained on the disk. Pay the authors, and they'll support you.

The Programs

Here, in alphabetical order, are all the programs you'll find on the disk. Enjoy!

AppDisk 1.5

Mark Adams
America Online MarkA38

AppDisk is a RAM disk utility. To use it, simply double-click the AppDisk icon. AppDisk will make a RAM disk of whatever RAM size the application is currently set to use. You can change this amount in the Get Info box for AppDisk in the Finder. (See chapter 4 for more details.)

BNDL Banger v.1.2

Tim Swihart
P.O. Box 160643
Cupertino, CA 95016
Freeware ($7 for BNDL Banger Pro)

BNDL Banger is a drag-and-drop application. You use it by dragging a program—generally something you just created—onto it, and then restarting your Mac. The program's unique icon will then be used by the Finder. (See chapter 4 for more details.)

DebugWindow 1.4
Keith Ledbetter
Freeware
America Online: Kledbetter

To use DebugWindow, youll need to add an XCMD to your HyperCard stack, or link in the C code library included with the program. (See chapter 8 for more details.)

Disinfectant
John Norstad
email j-norstad @ nwu.edu
Freeware

Disinfectant is an application—simply double-click the icon to run it.The Scan button will scan your hard disk for viruses. You can also have Disinfectant install an extension that watches for viral activity all the time. (See chapter 2 for more details.)

Extensions Manager 2.0.1
Ricardo Batista
Freeware

This extension will let you turn on or off other extensions. Its priceless when you're trying to track down an extension conflict. To install it, place Extensions Manager in your Control Panel folder. (See chapter 3 for more details on extensions.)

File Buddy 2.0.6
Laurence Harris
1100 West Highway
54 Bypass Apt.29J
Chapel Hill, NC 27516-2826
America Online: Lharris
$25

B

This drag-and-drop application displays a dialog box filled with file information, much of which you probably never even knew existed. Just drag a file onto it and it works its magic. (See chapter 4 for more details.)

GTQ Scripting Library 1.0

Gregory T. Quinn
AppleLink D3297
Internet: gtql@cornell.edu
Freeware

GTQ Scripting Library adds over 40 new commands to AppleScript. You must have already installed AppleScript for this package to work. Add these files into your Scripting Additions folder, inside your Extensions folder. They will be usable the next time you run a Script Editor. (See chapter 5 for more details.)

Hells Programmer Font 1.1

Paul Cunningham
P.O. Box 1923
Mango, FL 33550-1923
CompuServe: 75020,3540

This is a great font for programmers. For System 7.1, drop the font file into your Font folder inside your System folder. For System 7, drop the font file onto your System suitcase file inside your System folder. (See chapter 4 for more details.)

LaunchFile XCMD Source

David B. Lamkins
Freeware

This is source code: use it, read it, learn it, know it. You'll need at least a text editor to read it. If you want to compile the XCMD yourself, you'll need a Pascal compiler (either Think, MPW, or Code Warrior will do nicely.) (See chapter 7 for more details.)

Mercutio 1.1.4

Raymon M. Selciano
CompuServe: 76166,3627
Applelink: SUMMIT
Freeware

Mercutio is an MDEF that allows you to use shift- and
option-command key combinations to activate menu items.
You can add this MDEF to your own programs for a real
professional look. Refer to the documentation that
accompanies this file for usage information.(See chapter 7
for more details.)

PocketForth 6.3

Chris Heilman
CompuServe: 70566,1474
America Online: cheilman

Pocket Forth is a great way to get started learning the
programming language Forth. Start this Forth interpreter by
double-clicking its icon. (See chapter 6 for more details.)

Reference Link

James W. Walker
CompuServe 76367,2271

Place this in your Extensions folder. When you
command-option click on any word in any text editing
window, it will attempt to look up that word in the Think
Reference databse. Please note that this requires Think
Reference, which is a commercial product available from
Symantec. (See chapter 4 for more details on Think
Reference.)

ROMmie 1.0

Rolan M
roland.mansson@ldc.lu.se
Freeware

B

When you run ROMmie, it will create a copy of the resources inside your Mac's ROMs. It generates a file you can open with ResEdit. (See chapter 4 for more details.)

StuffIt Expander
Leonard Rosenthol, Aladdin Systems, Inc.
Freeware

To decompress Stuffit or Compactor Pro archives, AppleLink packages, or BinHex files, drag them onto the Stuffit Expander icon. (See chapter 2 for more details.)

Swatch 1.2.2
Joe Holt
Internet: jholt@adobe.com
America Online: Jholt
AppleLink: ADOBE.APDENG (attn: joe)

Run this application to see a graphical display of the memory usage of all running programs. (See chapter 8 for more details.)

System Errors 7.0.1
"Dr. Pete" Corless
Apple Computer
20525 Mariani Ave.
Cupertino, CA 95015
Freeware

This program displays a list of all System error codes. Simply double-click its icon in the Finder to see the list. (See chapter 8 for more details.)

TE32K 1.2
Roy Wood
122 Britannia Ave.
London, Ontario, N6H 2J5
CANADA
rrwood@canrem.com
rrwood@canrem.uucp
Freeware

This source code requires a C compiler, such as the Think, MPW, or CodeWarrior development environments. (See chapter 6 for more details.)

TIFFWindow 1.1
Robert Morris
P.O. Box 1044
Harvard Square Station
Cambridge, MA 02238
ecognome@aol.com
$2 for commercial distribution

This stack requires HyperCard version 2.0 or later. To use,double-click the program icon. The source code included requires a C compiler, such as the Think, MPW, or Code Warrior environments. (See chapter 5 for more details.)

UnZip 1.1.0
Samuel H. Smith
The Toolshop BBS
602-279-2673

The compression program PKZIP is big in the DOS/Windows world. If you need to decompress something in PKZIP format, simply drag it onto this icon. (See chapter 2 for more details.)

ZTerm
David P. Alverson
Compuserve 72155,1560

ZTerm is a terminal emulation program that you can use to connect with BBSs and commercial online services such as CompuServe Please refer to the documentation that accompanies this application for specific instructions regarding its use. (See chapter 2 for more details.)

B

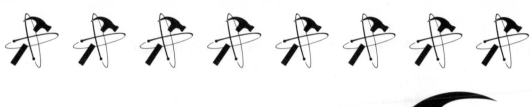

It Came From the Internet, Kinda

Remember when I said in Chapter 1 that there were lots of great people out there solving all your problems for you? Well, here's where that happens. This appendix contains the entire FAQ (or Frequently Asked Questions) file for the usenet newsgroup "comp.sys.mac.programmer." When I was just starting out, I learned quite a bit from documents like these.

Although it was never the intention of this book to teach readers how to program, I knew I would be remiss if I didn't at least address the basic questions: How do I get started? Where can I turn for help? Why does my GWorld code always crash? Well, I can't help you with the last one, but for the other questions, look no further.

Network in the raw

This appendix is totally internet-verité If you logged onto the internet and downloaded this file, this is exactly what you'd see. It's like that raw brown sugar for folks who think processed sugar is bad for them. The internet is a raw, unrefined place. I wanted to provide you with a safe, friendly environment for meeting the kind of in-your-face help the net provides.

See what you can glean from this, and if you need more, surf the newsgroup. You'll be amazed what you can find.

A big hearty thanks goes out to Jon W{tte, who provided this file.

Archive-name: macintosh/programming-faq

The Public Domain Mac Programming FAQ Answer sheet.

Last update: 931023

This sheet was started by and is presently maintained by Jon W{tte, whom you may reach as h+@nada.kth.se. If there is anything you find errant, missing, or in need of an update, please send me your submission and I will include it (I can't promise correct attributions, but I will try). All FAQ Answer submissions sent to me will be considered to be in the public domain unless stated otherwise (in which case they will not be included in this FAQ sheet).

This sheet is currently archived on nada.kth.se where you can reach it using afs as /afs/nada.kth.se/public/ftp/pub/hacks/mac-f aq/CSMP_PD_FAQ or using anonymous FTP (GIVE YOUR E-MAIL ADDRESS AS PASSWORD!) as pub/hacks/mac-faq/CSMP_PD_FAQ.

I will try to update this sheet every three weeks or so. Changes since first revision:

Fixed spelling and formatting. Added question numbering.
Files and Networks: [Mattias Ullrich]
Lisp and SmallTalk: [Rainer Joswig]
Free development languages: [Bob Loewenstein]
Various: [Pete Gontier]
Lots of suggestions: [Lewis]
Wake Up And Smell The Glue: [Matthias Neeracher]
Development environments: [Howard Berkey]
SmallTalk: [Alun ap Rhisiart]
CustomGetFile: [Jim Walker]

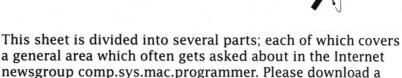

This sheet is divided into several parts; each of which covers a general area which often gets asked about in the Internet newsgroup comp.sys.mac.programmer. Please download a copy of this answer sheet and search it before you post to the 'net, to help reduce bandwidth.

There is NO or VERY LIMITED error checking in these code examples, FOR BREVITY ONLY. You should make sure you ALWAYS check ALL return codes, and handle any that you are not prepared to deal with appropriately.

The coding style used in the example C code is my own, and you'll have to live with it.

The groups are (you may search for *<number>* to jump directly to a group with its questions and answers)

0) Development and debugging tools and documentation for the Mac
1) Files and the File Manager
2) Serial ports
3) TCP/IP and sockets
4) AppleEvents and the Apple Object Model
5) AppleScript
6) Drawing using QuickDraw
7) Drawing NOT using QuickDraw (aka directly to screen)
8) Cache issues and other processor differences
9) What about pre-emptive multitasking?
10) Handles; they are driving me crazy; Memory issues
11) _Gestalt and compatibility
12) Standalone code and dynamic linking
13) Reading the keyboard for games and screen savers
14) QuickTime
15) Ice Cream and Frozen Yoghurt

C

0 Development and debugging tools for the Macintosh

0.1) Q: What do I need to start writing Macintosh software?

A: A Mac, a lot of time, and a few hundred $. Although you can develop software on a Classic-type machine, it is not to be attempted by the weak of heart or stressed of time. If you're doing paid work and/or work for a company, a Quadra-class machine or Centris 650 or better is almost a must; remember that your time costs your employer much more than just your salary. 8 MB is a minimum to run at all comfortably, and Virtual Memory is not suited for development work. Similarly, if you don't have at least 20 MB free on your hard disk (40 MB for MPW), you need to buy more space.

You need a development system such as Think C, Think Pascal , MPW C or Prograph, you need at least some of the New Inside Mac books (Toolbox Essentials, Files, Memory come to mind) and a good entry-level third-party book may help.

Once you are up to speed on the general layout of the Mac and its toolboxes, you should call APDA and order the monthly developer mailing, which will give you a CD chock full of documentation, utilities, and system software once a month. You will also, obviously, need a CD player; one of which Apple's own CD300 is a very good buy at the time of writing this. If you don't have the dough for the monthly mailing ($250/year) you can order a _develop_ subscription; this quarterly magazine ($30-$50/year) comes with a CD containing all Inside Mac documentation.

Another tool which many find a must-have is the Think Reference version 2.0, containing reference material on the most used parts of the Mac toolbox with lightning-fast look-up and mostly correct usage hints and code snippets.

0.2) Q: What is the most used Macintosh development language?

A: Out of products on the market, I have no idea; both MPW and Think products appear to be used. Among hobbyists, the Think products from Symantec are most popular because of the low price, and steep educational discounts, and, of course, the easily approachable interface!

The Think C linker only strips dead code on a FILE level basis (and this is when you turn on "Smart Linking"). The MPW linker (of no specified IQ, as someone so eloquently put it :-) strips dead code by the function. That may be part of the reason the Think C linker is ten times faster than the MPW linker.

In the beginning, the Mac was programmed using Mc68000 assembly or Pascal; this was reflected in the Old Inside Mac volumes which only gave Pascal-style and assembly-style interfaces to the Mac toolbox. These days, Apple tells us to use C or even better C++ for developing new applications, as that will speed up the transition to PowerPC and also coming cross-platform efforts.

There are also at least two Fortran compilers, at least three SmallTalk implementations (ObjectWorks, SmallTalk/V and SmallTalkAgents), a world-class LISP/CLOS implementation (Macintosh Common Lisp 2.0), and a Modula/2 implementation. Apparently, using Envy/packager, you can strip out unused code pretty effectively from Digitalk and PP apps, which are then smaller (and of course more memory efficient) than C++ apps.

Metrowerks have a Pascal and a Modula II compiler. Rumour has it they're building C and C++ for both 68K and coming PPC Macs.

CSI has MacForth, of which I only know the name and someone who says it's pretty good.

There is another good Common Lisp implementation: Procyon Common Lisp. I don't know if it is actively supported, but Procyon CL is also available for DOS, OS/2 and Windows (as Allegro CL/PC) and actively developed.

0.3) Q: Where do I find a public domain C compiler for the Mac. Is there a GCC for the mac? What about the FSF boycott of Apple products?

A: There is no really good solution for a "for-free" C development system for the Mac. GCC has been ported, but requires the MPW shell and MPW assembler to run; these have to be bought from APDA. There is a standalone port of GCC 1.37 underway, but it is presently on hold because of licensing issues. There was a freely available C compiler called Harvest C, which was somewhat unstable but usable for smaller programs; it was abandoned by the original author Eric W. Sink because of a lack of time.

The FSF boycott of Apple products means they will not talk to you if you ask them for help in doing a Mac port, and they will not incorporate your changes into their main code base. However, they still allow others to port GNU stuff to the Mac, and it has been done with most of the application-like GNU programs (bison, flex, perl (not really part of GNU), ...)

0.4) Q: Are there any other free Mac development platforms?

A: Yerk and Mops. These are object-oriented languages based on the old product Neon which itself was based on Forth. They are available with Manuals at oddjob.uchicago.edu (anonymous FTP).

Plus, there's MacGambit, MacScheme, xlisp, and MacMETH which is the actual ETH (read: Nick Wirth's group) Modula 2, all for free via FTP.

And OpenProlog. And SIOD (Scheme in One Defun) And [mail in more if you dare]

0.5) Q: What's the difference between the MPW and Think environments?

A: The main difference is that Think is an integrated environment, while MPW provides you with a command-line shell for your Mac and tools to use in it. MPW also has a slightly higher systems demand and a much slower linker.

The good thing about MPW is that you can write scripts and make files to do anything you want in the way you want it.

Think still doesn't have a viable solution to do a build that requires more than one link operation, or has more than one destination file.

For the MPW environment, there are three source level debuggers; SADE, SourceBug, and Voodoo Monkey. The latter is an experimental debugger with support for threads debugging; the middle is bundled with MPW while SADE has to be bought separately (but is fully scriptable in its own scripting language).

The Think environments have their own integrated debuggers; the Think Pascal one has a lot of useful features while the Think C/C++ one is a little more basic (but is gaining in functionality with each release). Stepping through source code and looking at variables is generally faster and easier in Think than in the MPW debuggers.

Any commercial Mac developer should have both Think and MPW of whatever language they prefer (Pascal, C or C++).

0.6) Q: What is a good low-level debugger for the Mac?

A: MacsBug is freely available for ftp from ftp.apple.com; log in as user anonymous and give your FULL e-mail address as password. MacsBug is your basic monitor-type debugger that takes a few hundred Ks of memory, and lets you break, step, disassemble, look at the stack, etc. of most anything running on your Mac. Since it's free (it's also on the developer CDs) and provides most of the functionality you need, this is a popular choice.

TMON is another debugger which sports a more mac-like interface; it provides windows and uses the mouse. It can take as little or as much memory as you want by excluding or including certain areas of functionality. A nice touch is the 6502 disassembler that you can use to debug the code the IOP processors run on the Mac IIfx and Quadra 900/950.

Jasik Designs have a debugger called The Debugger which can do both low- and high-level debugging, with or without source and for all types of code, application, code resources, everything. This is the debugger of choice for many large developers because of its high power and many features not found anywhere else. However, newcomers beware! This is the Lamborghini of debuggers; if you know how to drive it, it is the fastest way from A to B; if you don't, you'll just end up in the ditch.

0.7) Q: Are there any visual developments environments for the Mac (comparable to Visual C++)?

A: There is no Visual C++ as such. However, there is a C++ parser/editor called ObjectMaster which provides good browsing and editing capabilities if you already have a C++ compiler. Think C++ also comes with a browser built-in, and you can draw dialogs/windows using plain old ResEdit, even for your custom view types.

AppMaker is a GUI builder/code generator. Granted, it's not as nice as VC++, but it's quite a product in any case.

Also, Neuron Data has their UI tool called Open Interface, which is better than VC++ and creates code portable across 35 platforms. Unfortunately it's $2500 per developer per platform. (There's also two other cross-platform products called XVT and Galaxy; the former has gotten flak on UseNet while the latter reportedly has decent networking support.)

There is a fully visual, dynamic, object-oriented data-flow-drive.

n programming language for the Mac called Prograph Corporate Programming Something-or-other (CPX). It is expensive ($1500) but offers a built-in database, easy interfaces to existing data bases, very high productivity in implement-test-debug cycling and also offers cross-platform capabilities (it comes with a class library which, when your code is written using it, works under Windows after re-compilation.)

There is a crossing between SmallTalk and C++ that is called Component Workshop; although it seems large and slowly evolving, it does offer some promising features not found in C++ itself.

There is also something called SmallTalkAgents that makes it easy to create Mac applications using SmallTalk. If you'd rather do Common Lisp, Macintosh Common Lisp offers a Common Lisp Object System with support for most Mac interface items; you can edit code while it is running and build standalone applications.

However, all of these tools generate rather larger binaries with larger system demands than a program written in C. On the other hand, C++ programs require more memory and disk space than programs written in assembly. It's a trade-off, and I believe this type of tools is the wave of the near future.

0.8) Q: What class libraries are there for the Mac?

A: Apart from the libraries mentioned above, there are three contenders: MacApp, TCL, and OOPC. On the horizon may be Bedrock.

MacApp is a heavy-duty class library that has tons of features and a steep learning curve; it runs under MPW with Pascal or C++, and also under Think Pascal 4.0. A major application written in MacApp is PhotoShop.

TCL stands for Think Class Library and comes with Think Pascal, C, or C++. It is a smaller library that still fills most peoples' needs; since Think C implements a subset of C++ (the most important OO concepts such as virtual functions and inheritance) and the TCL is carefully written not to take advantage of any C++ features not in Think C, you can use it with Think C. A major application written in TCL is Lotus 1-2-3.

OOPC is a newcomer in the field, and uses plain ANSI C. However, it mangles the pre-processor to provide you with a system with full inheritance, virtual functions, and dynamic re-binding of functions for classes or individual objects. Start-up is slow, since all "linking" of virtual functions and classes is made at run-time, but performance otherwise is good. A Windows version is promised for later this year.

0.9) Q: How should I debug and test my software?

A: Get ahold of, and install, the extensions DoubleTrouble, DisposeResource, and EvenBetterBusError. They will catch 80% of any memory-related bugs you may have, including many bugs that follow NULL handles or pointers.

C

A low-level debugger is required, and while you install it, install the "leaks" dcmd which will help you catch memory leaks in your application. All of these tools are available from ftp.apple.com.

1 Files and the File Manager

1.1) Q: How do I tell fopen() to open a file the user has selected using StandardGetFile?

A: The "standard" ANSI C file functions are less than well suited for the Macintosh way of doing things. However, if you are doing a port for your own enjoyment and benefit (or maybe for in-house work) you can use the following function (see below about converting a wdRefNum into a vRefNum/parID pair):

```
*code*
FILE *
fopen_mac ( short vRefNum , long parID , char * fileName , char
* mode ) {
short oldVol ;
short aVol ;
long aDir , aProc ;
FILE * ret = NULL ;
   if ( GetVol ( NULL , & oldVol ) ) { return NULL ;
   }
if ( GetWDInfo ( oldVol , & aVol , & aDir , & aProc ) )
{ return NULL  ;
      }
   if ( HSetVol ( NULL , vRefNum , parID ) ) {
       return NULL ;
   }
   ret = fopen ( fileName , mode ) ;
   if ( HSetVol ( aVol , aDir ) ) {
      /* an error we can't currently handle */
   }
   if ( SetVol ( oldVol ) ) {
      /* an error we can't currently handle */
   }
   return ret ;
}
*end*
```

All of the above is necessary for one reason or another—if you are interested, by all means look HSetVol up in Think Reference 2.0 or New Inside Mac: Files.

In older versions of MPW this wouldn't work since the MPW libraries used to do a GetVol and explicitly use that value by itself.

1.2) Q: When can I use the HOpen, HCreate, etc. file calls? Are they only System 7 calls?

A: All the HXxx calls that take a vRefNum and parID as well as the file name are implemented in glue that works on any system that has HFS (meaning 3.2 and up with the HD20 INIT, and all systems from System 6 and up).

The glue is available in MPW 3.2 and up, and Think C 5.0 and up. This goes for all HXxx calls except HOpenDF; therefore, if you are interested in System 6 compatibility, use HOpen instead and make sure you don't allow file names beginning with a period.

1.3) Q: Why do you say wdRefNum sometimes and vRefNum sometimes? Why do you say parID sometimes and dirID sometimes?

A: When the Mac first made an appearance in 1984, it identified files by using a vRefNum (volume reference number meaning a floppy disk or later hard disk) and a name. Once HFS saw the light of day, folders within folders became a reality, and you needed a dirID as well to point out what folder you really meant on the volume. However, older programs that weren't being rewritten still knew nothing about directory IDs, so Apple had SFGetFile make up "fake" vRefNums that didn't just specify a volume, but also a parent folder. These are called wdRefNums (for working directory) and were a necessary evil invented in 1985. You should not create (or, indeed, use) wdRefNums yourself.

There is a system-wide table that maps wdRefNums onto vRefNum/parID pairs. There is a limit to the size of this table. A dirID and a parID is almost the same thing; you say "parID" when you mean the folder something is in, while you say a "dirID" when you mean the folder itself. If you, for instance, have a folder called "Foo" with a folder called "Bar" in it, the parID for "Bar" would be the dirID for "Foo."

1.4) Q: How do I convert a wdRefNum as returned by SFGetFile into a vRefNum/parID pair to use with the HXxx calls.
A: Use GetWDInfo, which is declared as:

> Pascal OSErr GetWDInfo (short wdRefNum , short * vRefNum , long * parID , OSType * procID) ;

The procID parameter must be non-NULL and point to an OSType variable, but the value of that variable can and should be ignored.

It is recommended that, as soon as you get your hands on a wdRefNum, for instance from SFGetFile, you directly convert it into a vRefNum/parID pair and always use the latter to reference the folder.

1.5) Q: How do I select a folder using SFGetFile?
A: This requires a custom dialog with a filter proc. It is too complicated to show here, but not totally impossible to comprehend. There is sample code on ftp.apple.com, in the directory dts/snippets, on how to do this.

1.6) Q: How do I get the full path of a file referenced by a vRefNum, parID, and name?
A: You don't.

OK, I cheated you. There is exactly ONE valid reason to get the full path of a file (or folder, for that matter) and that is to display its location to the user in, say, a settings dialog. To actually save the location of the file you should do this (assuming the file is in an FSSpec called theFile—you can use FSSpecs in your program even if you don't run under System 7; just make your own MyFSMakeFSSpec that fills in the FSSpec manually if it's not implemented):

```
*code*
if ( ! aliasManagerAvailable ) { /* System 6 ? */
```

```
GetVolumeName ( theFile -> vRefNum , vName ) ; GetVolumeModDate
( vRefNum , & date ) ;
Save ( vName , date , parID , fileName ) ;
} else {
NewAlias ( NULL , theFile , & theAlias ) ;
   Save ( theAlias ) ;
   DisposeHandle ( ( Handle ) theAlias ) ;
}
*end*
```

If you are really concerned about these issues (of course you are!) you should save BOTH of these methods when available, and load back whatever is there that you can handle, since users may be using your application in a mixed System 6/System 7 environment.

To get back to the file is left as an exercise for the reader.

To open a file using fopen() or the Pascal equivalent, see above about using and not using HSetVol.

1.7) Q: What about actually getting the full path for a file? I promise I will only use it to show the location of a file to the user!

A: Enter PBGetCatInfo, the Vegimatic of the Mac file system. Any Mac hacker of knowledge has taken this system call to his heart. What you do is this:

```
*code*
OSErr
GetFolderParent ( FSSpec * fss , FSSpec * parent ) {
CInfoPBRec rec ;
short err ;
   * parent = * fss ;
   rec . hFileInfo. ioNamePtr = parent -> name ;
   rec . hFileInfo. ioVRefNum = parent -> vRefNum ;
   rec . hFileInfo. ioDirID = parent -> parID ;
   if ( parent -> name [ 0 ] ) {
       rec . hFileInfo . ioFDirIndex = 0 ;
   } else {
       rec . hFileInfo . ioFDirIndex = -1 ;
   }
   rec . hFileInfo. ioFVersNum = 0 ;
   err = PBGetCatInfoSync ( & rec ) ;
if ( ! ( rec . hFileInfo . ioFlAttrib & 0x10 ) )
{ /* Not a folder */ if ( ! err ) {
```

```
            err = dirNFErr ;
        }
    }
    parent -> parID = rec . dirInfo . ioDrParID ;
    parent -> name [ 0 ] = 0 ;
    return err ;
}
OSErr
GetFullPathHandle ( FSSpec * fss , Handle * h )
{
    Handle  tempH = NULL ;
    short err ;
   FSSpec fs = * fss ;
   while ( fs . parID > 1 ) {
        tempH = NULL ;
PtrToHand ( & fs . name [ 1 ] , & tempH , fs . name [ 0 ] ) ;
PtrAndHand ( ( void * ) ":" ,
tempH , 1 ) ;
        HandAndHand ( * h , tempH ) ;
SetHandleSize ( * h , 0L ) ; HandAndHand ( tempH , * h ) ;
DisposeHandle ( tempH ) ; tempH = NULL ;
GetFolderParent ( & fs , & sSpec ) ;
        fs = sSpec ;
    }
    GetVolName ( fs. vRefNum , fs . name ) ;
PtrToHand ( & fs . name [ 1 ] , & tempH , fs . name [ 0 ] ) ;
PtrAndHand ( ( void * ) ":" , tempH , 1 ) ;
    HandAndHand ( * h , tempH ) ;
    SetHandleSize ( * h , 0L ) ;
    HandAndHand ( tempH , * h ) ;
    DisposeHandle ( tempH ) ;
    tempH = NULL ;
    if ( ! IsFolder ( fss ) ) {
    SetHandleSize ( * h , GetHandleSize ( * h )  - 1 ) ;
// Remove colon }
    return 0 ;
}
*end*
```

1.8) Q: So how do I get the names of the files in a directory?

A: You use PBGetCatInfo again, but this time you set ioFDirIndex to 1 or more (you need to know the dirID and vRefNum of the folder you're interested in). You then call PBGetCatInfoSync for values of ioFDirIndex from 1 and up, until you get an fnfErr. Any other err means you are not allowed to get info about THAT item, but you may be for the next. Then collect the names in the string you made ioNamePtr point to as you go along. Note that you need to fill in the ioDirID field for each iteration through the loop, and preferrably clear the ioFVersNum as well.

Note that the contents of a directory may very well change while you are iterating over it; this is most likely on a file server that more than one user uses, or under System 7 where you run Personal File Share.

1.9) Q: How do I find the name of a folder for which I only know the dirID and vRefNum?

A: You call (surprise!) PBGetCatInfo! Make ioNamePtr point to an empty string (but NOT NULL) of length 63 (like, an Str63) and ioFDirIndex negative (-1 is a given winner)—this makes PBGetCatInfo return information about the vRefNum/dirID folder instead of the file/folder specified by vRefNum, parID and name.

1.10) Q: How do I make the Finder see a new file that I created? Or if I changed the type of it, how do I display a new icon for it?

A: You call (surprise!) PBGetCatInfo followed by PBSetCatInfo for the FOLDER the file is in. In between, you should set ioDrMdDat to the current date&time. Code:

```
*code*
OSErr
TouchFolder ( short vRefNum , long parID ) {
CInfoPBRec rec ;
Str63 name ;
short err ;
rec . hFileInfo . ioNamePtr = name ; name [ 0 ] = 0 ;
rec . hFileInfo . ioVRefNum = vRefNum ; rec . hFileInfo .
ioDirID = parID ; rec .
FileInfo . ioFDirIndex = -1 ; rec . hFileInfo . ioFVersNum = 0
; err = PBGetCatInfo ( &
ec ) ;
 if ( err ) {
return err ;
 }
GetDateTime ( & rec . dirInfo . ioDrMdDat ) ; rec . hFileInfo .
ioVRefNum = vRefNum ;
rec . hFileInfo . ioDirID = parID ; rec . hFileInfo .
```

```
ioFDirIndex = -1 ; rec . hFileInfo .
ioFVersNum = 0 ;
    err = PBSetCatInfo ( & rec ) ;
    return err ;
}
*end*
```

1.11) Q: Aren't we done with PBGetCatInfo soon?

A: Well, it turns out that you can also find out whether an FSSpec is a file or a folder by calling PBGetCatInfo and check bit 4 (0x10) of ioFlAttr to see whether it is a folder. You may prefer to call ResolveAliasFile for this instead.

You can also check the script of the file's title using PBGetCatInfo and check the ioFlFndrXInfo field if you want to work with other script systems than the Roman system.

Another common use is to find out how many items are in a folder; the modification date of something or the correct capitalization of its name (since the Mac file system is case independent BUT preserves the case the user uses).

1.12) Q: How do I set what folder should initially be shown in the SFGetFile boxes?

A: You stuff the dirID you want to show into the lo-mem global CurDirStore, and the NEGATIVE of the vRefNum you want into the lo-mem global SFSaveDisk.

If you are using CustomGetFile and return sfSelectionChanged from an "init" message handler, you must remember to clear the script code, else the selection will not change.

1.13) Q: How do I find the folder my application started from? How do I find the application file that's running?

A: Under System 7, you call GetCurrentProcess, followed by GetProcessInformation with a pointer to an existing FSSpec in the parameter block. This will give you your file, and, by using the vRefNum and parID, the folder the application is in.

Beware from writing to your applications resource or data forks; the former breaks on CDs/write protected floppies/file servers/virus checkers, the latter fails on PowerPC as well as in the above cases.

2 Serial ports

2.1) Q: How do I get at the serial ports?

A: You call OpenDriver for the names "\p.AOut" and "\p.AIn" to get at the modem port, and "\p.BOut" and "\p.BIn" for the printer port. The function RAMSDOpen was designed for the original Mac with 128 KB of memory and 64 KB of ROM, and has been extinct for several years.

However, many users use their serial ports for MIDI, LocalTalk, graphic tablets, or what have you and have installed an additional serial port card to get more ports. What you SHOULD do as a good application is to use the Comms Toolbox Resource Manager to search for serial resources; this requires that the Comms Toolbox is present (true on earlier System 6 with an INIT, on later System 6 and System 7 always, as well as on A/UX) and that you have initialized the comms resource manager. The exact code follows (adapted from Inside Mac Comms Toolbox):

```
*code*
#include <CommsResources.h>
OSErr
FindPorts ( Handle * portOutNames , Handle * portInNames ,
Handle * names ,
Handle * iconHandles ) {
OSErr ret = noErr ;
short old = 0 ;
CRMRec theCRMRec , * found ; CRMSerialRecord * serial ;
* portOutNames = NewHandle ( 0L ) ; * portInNames = NewHandle (
0L ) ; *
names = NewHandle ( 0L ) ;
* iconHandles = NewHandle ( 0L ) ; while ( ! ret ) {
        theCRMRec . crmDeviceType = crmSerialDevice ;
        theCRMRec . crmDeviceID = old ;
        found = ( CRMRec * ) CRMSearch ( ( QElementPtr ) &
theCRMRec ) ;
    if ( found ) {
        serial = ( CRMSerialRec * ) found -> crmAttributes ;
        old = found -> crm DeviceID ;
PtrAndHand ( & serial -> outputDriverName , * portOutNames ,
```

C

```
sizeof (
serial -> outputDriverName ) ) ;
PtrAndHand ( & serial -> inputDriverName , * portInNames ,
sizeof ( serial
-> inputDriverName ) ) ;
     PtrAndHand ( & serial -> name , * names ,         sizeof (
serial -> name ) ) ;
PtrAndHand ( & serial -> deviceIcon , * iconHandles , sizeof (
serial ->
deviceIcon ) ) ;
     } else {
         break ;
     }
   }
   return err ;
}
*end*
```

This will create four handles with the driver names, device names, and driver icon handles for all of the available serial devices. Then let the user choose with a pop-up menu or scrolling list, and save the choice in your settings file.

You can use OpenDriver, SetReset, SetHShake, SetSetBuf, SerGetBuf, and the other Serial Manager functions on these drivers. To write to the serial port, use FSWrite for synchronous writes that wait until all is written, or PBWrite asynchronously for queuing up data that is supposed to go out but you don't want to wait for it. At least once each time through your event loop, you should call SerGetBuf on the in driver reference number you got from OpenDriver, and call FSRead for that many bytes—neither more nor less.

If you are REALLY interested in doing the right thing, you will use the Communications Toolbox Connection Manager instead; this will give you access to modems, direct lines, and networks of various kinds using the same API! Great for stuff like BBSes that may be on a network as well, etc. The Comms Toolbox also provides modularized terminal emulation and file transfer tools, although the Apple-supplied VT102 tool is pretty lame, as is the VT102 mode of the VT320 tool.

3 TCP/IP and sockets

3.1) Q: Where is a Berkley sockets library for the Mac?

A: There are some problems with that. MacTCP, the Mac Toolbox implementation of TCP/IP, doesn't have an API that looks at all like Berkley sockets. For instance, there is ONE paramater-block call to do a combined listen()/accept()/bind()—sort of. I have heard that there may be a socket library available by ftp from MIT but haven't seen it myself.

There is also a pretty good C++ TCP implementation called GUSI which is easily handled, and it also is callable from C using the Berkley socket API. Apart from TCP, it also handles "standard" Mac network protocols such as ADSP. The big disadvantage is that it is currently only implemented for MPW. The ftp site is nic.switch.ch, software/mac/src/mpw_c.

I can also recommend the Communications Toolbox; for the price of using an API that is simpler than the Berkley sockets, you get the benefit of being able to use any kind of connection (TCP tools are available). Novell and Wollogong offer commercial socket-like libraries.

3.2) Q: Where do I find MacTCP?

A: You can buy the MacTCP developers kit from APDA. It is also available on E T O, and if you want saner headers than those, try ftp to seeding.apple.com.

4 AppleEvents and the AppleEvent Object Model

4.1) Q: What are AppleEvents?

A: AppleEvents are a level-5 network protocol. If you are not familiar with the ISO network stack, this means it's a way of structuring sessions between network entities (programs) that is not dependent on the underlying protocol (such as PPC or TCP/IP). Despite being a network protocol, they can be very useful on Macs that are not on a network. In short, they provide applications with a comprehensive way to send arbitrary structured data to other applications (or themselves) which receive the events through their main event loop.

The AppleEvent Object Model is a way of looking at applications and the data they contain, and also a level-6 network protocol. You _can_ send AppleEvent Object Model data through AppleEvents (and the standard AppleEvents defined in the AppleEvent Registry use it) but you don't have to—unless you want to talk with other applications, of course, then the AEOM is a lingua franca.

4.2) Q: What are the four required AppleEvents?

A: There are four events your application really must implement if you want to sell it: the kCoreEventClass class, kAEOpenApplication, kAEQuitApplication, kAEOpenDocuments, and kAEPrintDocuments events IDs. When you support these events (or any AppleEvents) you will not get startup info through GetAppParams() anymore, unless you run under System 6 of course. The kAEOpenApplication event will be sent to you when the user double-clicks your app and it's not started yet. When receiving it, you can put up a new untitled window.

kAEOpenDocuments is sent when the user double-clicks your apps documents. Note that if the first AppleEvent you receive is a kAEOpenDocuments event, the user started your app by double-clicking its documents.

kAEPrintDocuments is sent when the user selects your documents and chooses "Print" in the Finder menu. If this is the first AppleEvent you receive, you should print the documents and then quit the application again; if you received a kAEOpenApplication or kAEOpenDocuments event before this, you should just print the documents and close them when you're done.

kAEQuitApplication is sent to you when the user chooses "Shutdown" or "Restart" from the Apple Menu. You should ask the user whether he wants to save any unsaved changed documents, and then quit unless the user presses Cancel.

Interestingly enough, you can use these four AppleEvents to send even to non-AE-aware applications, and the system will translate these events into fake menu selections for you.

A good way of shutting down the Finder is to send it a Quit AppleEvent. You should send a Quit AppleEvent to File Sharing Extension before you shut down the Finder, though; the FSE is found by looking for a process with the creator 'hhgg'.

4.3) Q: Are there any limits or trade-offs with AppleEvents?

A: As always, more power means more responsibility.

AppleEvents sent to applications on other Macs require authentification the first time they are sent. If the remote Mac allows Guests to link to programs, the INIT AutoGuest 2.0 might help (or the code solution that comes with it and you can build into your application).

In the first version of the AppleEvent manager, there was a total 64K limit on the size of data and overhead. This limit has been lifted with the version of the AppleEvent manager that comes with AppleScript.

AppleEvents require a lot of memory copying and handle resizing in their construction; this means that large AppleEvents may be slow in construction, especially when compared to a pure PPC Toolbox or ADSP/ASDSP link.

You should use your own application signature as event class for AppleEvents you make up, in order not to collide with anybody else. Other than that, you are free to make your own events for your own needs, though supporting the required events and at least a subset of the Core event suite will buy you a lot of functionality from within AppleScript. Especially important are the Get Current Selection and Set Current Selection events (which are really Get/Set Data on the contents of the current selection of the application).

The signature for your application SHOULD be registered with DTS to avoid conflicts; this is done through e-mail to DEVSUPPORT@AppleLink.Apple.Com and the form you use is located on the developer CDs and found on ftp.apple.com.

5 AppleScript

5.1) Q: How does AppleEvents interface with AppleScript?

A: AppleEvents are the meat and potatoes of AppleScript. If you support the AppleEvent Object Model from within your application, users can control you through AppleScript.

The first thing you should do is get ahold of Inside Mac: Interapplication Communication, and a copy of the AppleEvents Registry. The former tells you all you ever need to know about AppleEvents, while the latter is paramount for implementing the right standard events. If everybody uses the standard events, dynamic data interchange between any applications will become sweet reality!

Then there is the 'aete' resource which lets you put names on the events you support, so that users can "Open Terminology" on your application from within the Apple Script Editor and use the proper AppleScript commands in their scripts. The format of an aete resource is defined in Inside Macintosh: Interapplication Communication.

5.2) Q: Can I compile and run scripts from within my application?

A: Yes, this is very simple. There are toolbox calls for reading scripts, compiling scripts, and executing scripts. (OSACompile, OSAExecute). These are all documented in Inside Mac: Interapplication Communication.

5.3) Q: Is this a good way of getting a macro language almost for free?

A: "Good" is an understatement. Just let users write scripts, load them into menu items and go. Total systems integration in under a week, including adding support for the AEOM to your application.

There is source code for an application called "MenuScipter" on the developer CD which shows you how to do an application with all of the menus being AppleScript scripts.

6 Drawing using QuickDraw

6.1) Q: Why is CopyBits so slow?

A: It is not. It just requires some hand-holding to get good results. The main rules are: Make sure the source and destination pixMaps are of the same depth.

Make sure the front color is black and the back color is white.

Use srcCopy and don't use a masking region.

Copy to an unclipped window (the frontmost window).

Make sure the ctSeed values of the source pixMap and dest pixMap match.

Copying few and large pixMaps is faster than copying many and small ones. Icon-sized sprites count as small ones.

Make sure your source bitmap or pixelMap has the same alignment, when adjusted for the source and destination rect expressed in global screen coordinates. The necessary alignment is 32 bits (4 bytes), although 128 bit (16 byte) alignment is probably even better on 68040 macs and won't hurt on other macs.

Example of global alignment:

Your window is positioned at (42,100) (H,V)

Your destination rectangle is (10,20)-(74,52)

The alignment coefficient of the rectangle in global coordinates is (42+10)*bitDepth where bitDepth is one of 1,2,4,8,16 or 32.

Make sure your source pixmap rect has the same coeffecient modulo as your alignment factor (in bits). For black&white macs, this is still true, although bitDepth is fixed at 1. Offscreen pixMaps can calculate with a "global position" of 0,0 and get correct results.

6.2) Q: Why is CopyBits still too slow?

A: Because there is always some overhead involved in calling QuickDraw; you have the trap dispatcher, clipping checks, and checking whether the CopyBits call is being recorded in a PICT handle (if you called OpenPicture).

If you can't live with this, look at *7* below, but PLEASE try and make CopyBits work, and retain the CopyBits code in your application, so users with special monitors (accellerator cards, PowerBook color screens, Radius Pivot screens) can still play your game. (Non-game applications don't need more speed than CopyBits can give at its max. Promise!)

6.3) Q: What is the fastest way to set one pixel?

A: NOT SetCPixel()! Assuming you have the correct ForeColor() set, you can set the pen size to (1,0) and call Line (0,1)

I have heard PaintRect is good for this but requires slightly more code. Using PaintRect eliminates a trap call.

6.4) Q: Why do pictures I record suddenly draw as empty space or not draw at all?

A: When recording pictures, you have to set the clipping area to exactly the frame of the picture you are recording. This is because it is initally set at -32768,32727 in both directions, and offsetting the picture even one pixel when drawing it will result in the region wrapping around and becoming empty.

When recording pictures, do this:

```
*code*
PicHandle h = OpenPicture ( & theRect ) ; ClipRect ( & theRect
) ;
    /* draw the picture */
    ClosePicture ( ) ;
*end*
```

6.5) Q: Where can I find the format of picture files and resources?

A: The format of a picture resource version 1 is defined in a technical note. This format is obsolete.

The format of a picture resource version 2 is defined in Old Inside Mac vol V, with addenda in Old Inside Mac vol VI.

Some things happen with QuickTime compressed pictures; try the Inside Mac: QuickTime book or wait for Inside Mac: Imaging which is the definitive reference on QuickDraw.

The format of a picture file is the same as that of a picture resource with 512 added 0 bytes in front.

6.6) Q: GWorlds?

A: What about them? They're great. Look them up in Old Inside Mac vol VI. Don't forget to SetGWorld back to what it was before calling WaitNextEvent.

6.7) Q: How do I find the current depth of the screen?

A: My question to you is: What screen? Many macs have more than one screen attached. You can use GetDeviceList and walk the devices to find the screen you're looking for (use TestDeviceAttrib to see whether it's a screen) or you can call GetMaxDevice() to find the deepest device your window intersects.

Once you have the device handle, finding the depth is just a matter of looking at the dgPMap pixMapHandle, and dereference it to the pmSize field. Done.

7 Drawing directly to screen

7.1) Q: Why is it a bad idea to draw directly to screen?

A: Because of several reasons:

- You will be incompatible with future display hardware.

- You will be incompatible with some present-day display hardware, such as Radius Pivots and PowerBook color screens.

- You have to think about a lot of things; testing it all on your own machine is not possible and the chances of crashing are great.

- You will be incompatible with future hardware where devices may live in some unaccessible I/O space.

7.2) Q: But I really need to do it. I can't make my animation into a QuickTime movie, and CopyBits is too slow, even when syncing to the screen retrace.

You have to prepare yourself, and ask these questions:

1. Do I want to support all screens, or just 8-bit devices?

2. Do I have a few weeks of free time to make it work?

3. Do I want to get nasty mail when I break on some hardware and have to rev the application—even if I may not be able to get ahold of the hardware that makes it break?

If all you're doing is rendering an image pixel-by-pixel or line-by-line, maybe you can draw directly into an offscreen pixMap/GWorld and then CopyBits the entire GWorld to screen? That will be more compatible, especially if you use the keepLocal flag when creating the GWorld.

7.3) Q: Okay, so how do I get the base address of the screen?

A: "The" screen? Which screen? There may be several. The base address may be on an accellerated screen card. There may be more than one screen covering the same desktop area.

Due to unfortunate circumstances, there is a bug in GetPixBaseAddr() that causes it to return incorrect results for some versions of System 7. Instead, get the baseAddr directly from the gdPMap handle of the GDHandle for the screen you draw to. This address may need switching to 32-bit mode to be valid.

7.4) Q: Quit stalling and give me code!

A: Okay, but I'll let you sweat over Inside Mac to figure out what it does. All of it is important, believe me! To make this code run faster, a lot of the things it does can be done once before starting to draw.

Make sure that you have a window that covers the area where you are drawing, so other windows will not be

overdrawn. Also make sure that you do not do
direct-to-screen-drawing while you are in the background.

```
*code*
/* This is presently untested code */
/* value is dependent on what depth the screen has */
/* this code doesn't work on non-color-quickdraw Macs */
/* (i e the MacClassic) */
/* where is in GLOBAL coordinates */
void
SetPixel ( Point where , unsigned long value ) {
Rect r ;
GDHandle theGD ;
char * ptr ;
long rowBytes ;
short bitsPerPixel ;
PixMapHandle pmh ;
Boolean oldMode ;
 r . left = where . h ;
 r . top = where. v ;
 r . right = r . left + 1 ;
r . bottom = r . top + 1 ;
 theGD = GetMaxDevice ( & r ) ;
 if ( theGD ) {
where . v -= ( * theGD ) -> gdRect . left ; where . h -= ( *
theGD ) -> gdRect . top ; pmh
= ( * theGD ) -> gdPMap ;
rowBytes = ( ( * pmh ) -> rowBytes ) & 0x3fff ; ptr = ( char *
) ( * pmh ) -> baseAddr ;
bitsPerPixel = ( * pmh ) -> pixelSize ; oldMode = true32b ;
          ptr += where . v * rowBytes ;
SwapMMUMode ( & oldMode ) ; switch ( bitsPerPixel ) { case 1 :
if ( value & 1 ) {
ptr [ where . h >> 3 ] |= ( 128 >> ( where . h & 7 ) ) ;
               } else {"
                  ptr [ where . h >> 3 ] &= ( 128 >> ( where . h & 7 ) ) ;
               }
               break ;
               case 2 :
     ptr [ where . h >> 2 ] &= ( 192 >> 2 * ( where . h & 3 )
) ;
ptr [ where . h >> 2 ] |= ( value & 3 ) << 2 * ( 3 - ( where .
h & 3 ) ) ; break ;
     case 4 :
           ptr [ where . h >> 1 ] &= ( where . h & 1 ) ? 0xf : 0xf0 ;
ptr [ where . h >> 1 ] |= ( value & 15 ) << 4 * ( 1 - ( where .
h & 1 ) ) ; break ;
```

```
      case 8 :
          ptr [ where . h ] = value ;
          break ;
      case 16 :
( ( unsigned short * ) ptr ) [ where . h ] = value ;
            break ;
          case 32 :
( ( unsigned long * ) ptr ) [ where . h ] = value ;
            break ;
      }
      SwapMMUMode ( & oldMode ) ;
  }
}
*end*
```

8 Cache issues and other processor differences

8.1) Q: Why does my application work on an SE with accellerator (or a Mac II or Quadra), but not on one without?

A: Assuming you're not calling Color QuickDraw (which is not available on accellerated SEs), you most probably have an odd-aligned word access somewhere.

The 68000 does not allow words or longwords to be read from odd addresses, while the 68020 and up relaxes this restriction (it still is slower than aligned-word access though).

This may or may not crash depending on your compiler:

```
*code*
struct foo {
 char c1 ;
 char c2 ;
 char c3 ;
 char c4 ;
 char c5 ;
} bar ;
    long * x = ( long * ) & bar . c2 ;
    * x = 0x12345678 ; /* X is odd if compiler doesn't pad */
This WILL crash on an SE/Plus/Classic/PB100:
char foo [ 10 ] ;
 long * x = ( long * ) & foo [ 1 ] ;
 * x = 0x12345678 ;
*end*
```

8.2) Q: Why does my application work on a IIci but not on a Quadra?

A: Two reasons:

1. The Quadras 900 and 950 have special processors that handle the serial ports; if you write directly to the serial chips, you will crash (this goes for the IIfx as well).

2. The Quadras have 68040 processors, as have the Centrises. These processors have separate instruction and data caches (like the 68030) but they are larger (4K each) and unlike the 68030 which is write-through data cached, the 68040 is copy-back data cached. This means that changes you make to "your code" aren't really changed all the time, since the changes may still be in the data cache and not written to memory when the CPU reads that part of memory into its I-cache. Even worse; that part might already have been read into the I-cache before you change it in the D-cache, meaning that writing out the D-cache will still not be enough. You need to flush both the caches when writing self-modifying code.

Self-modifying code includes code that builds its own jump tables and code that decrypts itself and code that "stubs" MDEFs or WDEFs to jump back into the application code.

You flush the cache using FlushDataCache() which is implemented if Gestalt says you have a 68020 or better processor (or if the _HwDispatch trap is implemented).

8.3) Q: Why does my application work on my Quadra but not on my accellerated SE?

A: You're probably calling Color QuickDraw without first checking if it's available. The following machines do not have color QuickDraw in ROM nor RAM:

Mac Plus, Mac SE, Mac Classic, Mac Luggable, PowerBook 100, Outbound

8.4) Q: I do check for color quickdraw, but crash nevertheless.

A: _Gestalt lies under some versions of System 7; it says that non-color machines HAVE color QuickDraw when you test using the gestaltQuickdrawFeatures selector.

Instead, check the gestaltQuickdrawVersion selector; if it returns >= gestalt8BitQuickdraw then you can safely use gestaltQuickdrawFeatures, else you only have b/w QuickDraw.

8.5) Q: Why are there no C/C++ compilers that optimize for the Mc68040?

A: Beats me; optimizing for the 68040 can make programs up to 50% faster on that chip while still losing nothing, or very little (less than 10%) on older chips.

9 Inflammatory subjects

9.1) Q: What about pre-emptive multitasking?

A: To the user, the Mac multitasking method, which builds upon each application calling WaitNextEvent, GetNextEvent or EventAvail every so often and the Process Manager/MultiFinder switching applications only at such calls, is at least as good as preemptive multitasking, because the present system prioritizes user interface responsiveness over everything else. The only shortfall about this is formatting floppies, which locks up the Mac CPU. This is because the Mac floppy controller is really stupid, and would happen even if the Mac multitasked preemptively.

There IS "real" pre-emptive multitasking available for use in Mac applications; the expensive way is buying A/UX 3.0 which can have Mac applications written as UNIX processes; the cheap way is installing the Thread Manager which will allow you to create pre-emptive threads. However, the restrictions on those threads are the same as those on Time Manager tasks: don't call any function in an unloaded segment, and don't call QuickDraw or any toolbox call which may move memory (which are most ToolBox calls;

paradoxally, BlockMove is safe :-) as are, surprisingly, FSRead and FSWrite).

There are several problems with making the Mac OS preemptive, including apps that draw outside their windows or directly to screen, user dragging, and other issues.

9.2) Q: What about protected memory? I'm sick and tired of re-booting when my application crashes.

A: Write better software!

Or install The Debugger from Jasik Designs, which can provide your application with write-protection of critical parts of memory. This may only work for 030 Macs, though.

Making the Mac OS memory-protected is tricky, because applications expect to be able to write to low memory, the system heap, temporary memory, window lists, and even each other's heaps in some interapplication communication solutions that date back to before AppleEvents and the PPC Toolbox.

10 Handles—they are driving me crazy

10.1) Q: What is a handle?

A: A handle is a pointer to a pointer to something. However, it is more than that; creating a handle by taking the address of one of your own pointers does NOT create a handle; the Memory Manager will only deal properly with handles that are created using NewHandle or something that calls it (such as NewRgn or GetResource).

10.2) Q: When do I have to lock a handle?

A: The contents of a handle may move, and when they do, the pointer your handle is pointing to is changed to point to the new address so your handle is always valid. The toolbox may call the memory manager to allocate more memory pretty much anytime you call it (the toolbox) and when memory is allocated, your handle may move in memory. Don't dereference a handle into a pointer (or take the address of a field in a record a handle is double-pointing to) and then call the toolbox and expect the pointer to still be valid. The only way to ensure that the pointer will still be valid is to call HLock on the handle to lock it.

Use HGetState and HSetState to save & restore the "locked" state of a handle when you lock it.

10.3) Q: How do I dispose of Handles?

A: DisposeHandle (formerly called DisposHandle) once and ONLY once will do the trick. Trying to dispose of an already disposed Handle is an error. DoubleTrouble (see above) will catch such bugs when they do occur.

10.4) Q: What about resources?

A: Calling GetResource returns NULL if the resource is not found or there is not enough memory, else it returns a handle to the resource. This handle may be moved or locked like any other handle, but DO NOT call DisposeHandle to get rid of a resource handle—call ReleaseResource. DisposeResource (see above) will catch this kind of bug.

Remember that AddResource makes a resource handle out of an ordinary handle, and RmveResource or DetachResource makes an ordinary handle out of a resource handle. You cannot call AddResource with a resource handle; you have to DetachResource it first.

Resource handles are automagically disposed when the resource file they belong to is closed.

10.5) Q: I'm trying to use a largish array in Think C, but get a "code overflow" error. This is valid C, why doesn't it work?

A: The ANSI standard does not guarantee that any structure larger than 32767 bytes will be correctly handled. Because of historical constraints, the Mac memory model is built around several small blocks of size 32K or less; these are used both for code and global/static data. If you want to use more code or data, you have to turn on "far code" or "far data"—you still will not get around the restriction of 32K code or data per compiled file, though.

As opposed to, say, DOS or Windows, however, you can allocate as much memory as you want (and there is in the machine) and step through it using ordinary pointers; it's just that global and static data space is addressed off the A5 register using a 16bit displacement addressing mode in the 68000 processor.

11 _Gestalt and compatibility

11.1) Q: I see all these people call Gestalt without first checking whether it's implemented. Isn't that bad?

A: No; Gestalt and a few other traps (the HXxx file manager traps, and FindFolder) are implemented using glue so they do the right thing even if the trap is not implemented.

If you want to get rid of the glue, you can #define SystemSevenOrLater (and, using Think C/C++, re-pre-compile MacHeaders). However, then you will be responsible for checking for these features before you use them.

11.2) Q: What more functions are implemented in glue?

A: Wake Up and Smell the Glue! [by Matthias Neeracher]

How often have you wished you could use that cool new ToolBox call, but didn't want to make your application System 7 dependent? Well, it might be that you *could* in fact have used the call. Several traps are implemented in glue, that is, much of their functionality is linked into your application and thus available even if you are running under an old System.

This list applies to MPW 3.2 and should also be valid for the current version of Think C. If you find any inaccuracies, please report them to me. (neeri@iis.ee.ethz.ch)

FSOpen: Tries first OpenDF, then Open.

HOpenResFile: Full functionality emulated if trap not available

HCreateResFile: Full functionality emulated if trap not available

FindFolder: Under System 6, understands the following values for folderType and returns the System Folder for all of them:

kAppleMenuFolderType

kControlPanelFolderType

kExtensionFolderType

kPreferencesFolderType

kPrintMonitorDocsFolderType

kStartupFolderType

kSystemFolderType

kTemporaryFolderType

SysEnvirons: Full functionality emulated if trap not available

NewGestalt: Returns an error if not implemented

ReplaceGestalt: Returns an error if not implemented

Gestalt: The following selectors are always implemented:

vers mach sysv proc fpu

qd kbd atlk ram lram

11.3) Q: I have to support System 6, don't I?

A: It would be foolish to lock yourself out of the many benefits the System 7 API provides for software that you start to write now. Some of the System 6 and older things (likely SFGetFile and wdRefNums among others) will be phased out of the interfaces and lose support, especially on future platforms.

The installed base of System 7 is larger than that of System 6; this is not surprising because Apple has been shipping System 7 for several years with all new machines, including the LCII, Classic II, Performas, and Color Classic. Another argument is that newer computer owners (having System 7) are much more likely to buy new software than old computer owners who have systems that already do what they want them to.

The added work to support both System 6 and System 7 is significant; if you have the time and money you may want to do it, but only supporting System 6 and not System 7 is doomed to fail in the market of today.

Some may call this position subjective; I call it business sense based on market demographics. A rule of thumb may be that if you target color machines only, you can just as well demand System 7 as well.

12 Standalone code and dynamic linking

12.1) Q: I've got a CODE resource off in limboland (sometimes called the resource fork) and I want to open it... what do I do?

A: You open the file you have the code resource in, load the resource and lock it high (don't unlock it first, since someone else may be using it). Then you cast the handle to a function pointer, and call it normally.

Suppose your code resource is compiled as a SACD id 128, and is defined as:

```
*code*
long
main ( MyParams * params ) {
    switch ( params -> message ) {
    case messageInit :
            return init ( params ) ;
 ...
 }
 return 0L ;
}
*end*
```

Also suppose you already have the vRefNum, parID, and name of the resource file you want to use. Do this:

```
*code*
    setup_paramblock ( & the_params ) ;
    the_params . message = messageInit ;
```

```
refNum = HOpenResFile ( vRefNum , parID , name , fsRdPerm ) ;
if ( refNum < 1 ) {
        fail ( ResError ( ) ) ;
}
the_code = GetResource ( 'SACD' , 128 ) ;
HLockHi ( the_code ) ;
retval = ( * ( ( long ( * ) ( MyParams * ) ) StripAddress ( *
the_code ) ) ) ( & the_params ) ;
  ...
*end*
```

The StripAddress is important; if your app is running in 24-bit mode, the resource handle may contain tag bits and you don't want strange things to happen if the code resource switches into 32-bit mode (which QuickDraw may do, incidentally).

Exactly how you structure your calling conventions is up to you; there is no accepted standard (except for HyperCard XCMDs, but that is probably overkill for you).

13 Reading the keyboard for games and screen savers

13.1) Q: How do I read the modifier keys of the keyboard?

A: Just call EventAvail and check the event.modifiers field. Only works when you are in the foreground. You can also use GetKeys(), or (as a last resort) check the lo-mem global KeyMap directly.

14 QuickTime

14.1) Q: I want to write a Amiga QuickTime player and need the CODEC format details.

A: Although the structure of QuickTime movies is well documented in Inside Mac: QuickTime, the inner workings of the Apple compression modules is a trade secret that Apple will only license to you at great cost. Perhaps it's time for a freeware, cross-platform QuickTime codec?

15 Ice Cream and Frozen Yoghurt

15.1) Q: Dessert?

A: Honey Hill Farms Cookie Jar Frozen Yoghurt or
Haagen-Dazs Raspberry & Cream Ice Cream.

Hokey-Pokey icecream with chocolate sauce and (for those
who like their brain food firmer) Almond and Double
Chocolate CookieTime cookies!? [Denis Birnie]

—Jon W{tte, h+@nada.kth.se, Mac Hacker Deluxe—
"From now on I will re-label the EQ on the deck as Fizz
and Wobble instead of HF and LF."

C

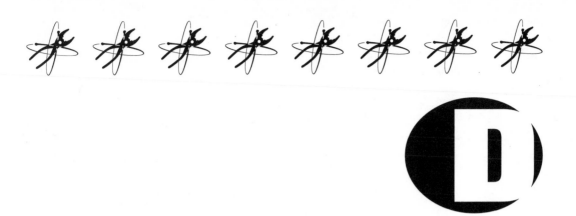

Local Heroes

While it may seem that I've stressed the importance of finding online friends to help you think through programming problems, don't forget the local factor. Most every community in the country (and many other countries) has a user group you can join.

Mac user groups used to rule the Mac universe. It was very satisfying to watch self-important tie-wearing MicroStuff employees kowtow to a crowd of geeks in t-shirts. Ah, those were the days.

The salad days of user groups may have passed, but they're still an important resource for anyone who uses computers. There are a whole host of niggling problems that a user group can help you solve—why isn't my network working? My printer uses the wrong fonts?—and so on. Yes, even you programmers, the top of the Mac food chain, will slam into these kinds of problems some day. Be humble and know where to turn for advice.

And importantly, the following user groups all have Programming Special Interest Groups. So if you need help with a programming problem—like, what do I pass to CopyBits?—you can ask the resident guru.

This list was provided by the User Group Connection (UGC). Thanks to Sam Decker for allowing us to reproduce it here. Note that the folks at the User Group Connection are nice enough to help you find the user group in your local area (and with a toll-free call!). Here's a short description of what the User Group Connection is all about and a list of user groups from across the country.

User Group Connection provides FREE support and benefits to computer user groups. UGC maintains the Apple Authorized User Group Database and Apple's User Group program. Benefits to user groups include monthly mailings full of vendor discounts and Apple product information, user group development support, the annual user group satellite T.V. show, quarterly videos, beta testing opportunities, MacWorld breakfasts, and much more.

To find a local Apple User Group in your area, call 1-800-538-9696. If you are interested in starting your own user group, and would like to register with the User Group Connection, call 408-461-5700. You can also reach User Group Connection at: 408-461-5701, Applelink: User.Groups, America Online: Apple UGC.

Alabama

Birmingham Apple Core
Birmingham, AL
205-967-4714

Macinsteins
Montgomery, AL
205-242-2670

Arizona

Mac Explorers
Phoenix, AZ
602-863-3763

Mountain View Computer Users Group
Sierra Vista, AZ
602-458-3042

Tucson Apple Core
Tucson, AZ
602-296-5491

Arkansas

Fayetteville Apple Users Group
Fayetteville, AR
501-442-7040

Pine Bluff Users Group
Pine Bluff, AR
501-535-2859

California

Almaden Apple II Users
San Jose, CA
408-997-3725

America Japan Macintosh Users Group
Los Altos, CA
415-949-5602

Apple Salinas Monterey User Group
Carmel, CA
408-424-2525

Applejacks Of The Inland Empire
San Bernardino, CA
714-864-2309

Hellenic User Group
Los Altos, CA
415-726-8738

Los Angeles Macintosh Group
Los Angeles, CA
310-278-5264

Mac Valley Users Group
Sherman Oaks, CA
818-784-2666

Mendocino Coast Macintosh Users Group
Comptche, CA
707-937-1002

D

North Coast Mac User Group
Santa Rosa, CA
707-887-7778

North San Diego Apple User Group
San Diego, CA
619-571-0757

Original Apple Corps
Los Angeles, CA
310-475-8400

Sierra Local User Group
Soulsbyville, CA
209-532-1419

So. California Electronic Mug
Cardiff By The Sea, CA

Colorado

Apple Three User Group
Highlands Ranch, CO
303-791-2077

Computer C.A.C.H.E./Tawug
Denver, CO
303-771-2019

Connecticut

Mac Owners, Users & System Enthusiasts
Monroe, CT
203-854-4109

Thames River Apple User Group
Gales Ferry, CT
203-464-9372

Delaware

Delaware Valley Apple Club For The Gs
Wilmington, DE
302-999-9282

Florida

Fort Walton Beach Apple Club
Fort Walton Beach, FL
904-862-3047

Mug Of Orlando
Winter Park, FL
407-275-1418

Pensacola Apple II Ug
Pensacola, FL
904-456-7096

S.W.A.C.K.S.
N. Fort Myers, FL
813-543-6329

Georgia

Boy Scout Troop 479-Golden Eagles Patrol
Marietta, GA
404-578-1344

Chattahoochee Mac Usergroup
Columbus, GA
205-480-9975

Idaho

Apple Boise User Group
Boise, ID
208-344-9506

North End Macintosh Users Group
Boise, ID
208-336-7890

D

Illinois

Hutsonville Computer Users Club
Hutsonville, IL
618-563-4912

Metroeast Macintosh Users Group
Belleville, IL
618-624-5776

Oswego Apple/Mac User Group
Oswego, IL
708-554-3444

Technological Renaissance Users Group
Marengo, IL
815-568-8751

Indiana

Lafayette Apple Forum: Toward Educating The Future
Lafayette, IN
317-474-1327

Iowa

Applecorp User Group Of Central Iowa
Stanhope, IA
515-826-3537

Bits & Pc's
Cresco, IA
319-547-5329

Kansas

Apple Tree User Group, Inc.
Hutchinson, KS
316-663-1582

Lawrence Apple User Group
Lawrence, KS
913-842-1172

Parsons Apple Users Group
Parsons, KS
316-421-6953

Kentucky

Eastern Kentucky Apple Users Group
Prestonsburg, KY
606-886-8044

Louisiana

Centenary Apple User Group
Shreveport, LA
318-742-7061

Chevron Macintosh Users Group
Slidell, LA
504-592-6748

Shreveport Area Macintosh User Group
Shreveport, LA
318-868-7997

Maine

Downeast Macintosh User Group
Woodland, ME
207-427-3325

Valley Computer Users Group
Kennebunkport, ME
207-967-8824

Maryland

Columbia Apple Slice
Columbia, MD
301-596-6443

Washington Apple Pi, Ltd.
Bethesda, MD
301-654-8060

Massachusetts

Boston Computer Society
Waltham, MA
617-290-5700

Michigan

Gateway Online Macintosh User Group
Livonia, MI
313-721-6070

Mactechnics-The Ann Arbor Computer Ug
Ann Arbor, MI
313-482-0501

Minnesota

Minnesota Apple Computer Ug
Hopkins, MN
612-229-6952

Missouri

Gateway Area Mac User Group
St. Louis, MO
314-664-6972

Nebraska

Apple Computer Enthusiasts
Omaha, NE
402-339-3590

Nevada

We The People Macintosh Users Group
Las Vegas, NV
702-258-0660

New Jersey

Amateur Computer Group Of NJ
North Brunswick, NJ
908-821-9063

Princeton Apple II User Group
Trenton, NJ
609-587-8334

South Jersey Apple Users Group
Cherry Hill, NJ
609-784-3028

New Mexico

Space Port Apple Users Group
Alamagordo, NM
505-434-1786

New York

Mac-Rug
Clinton, NY
315-792-9606

Macintosh Users Group Of Syracuse
Syracuse, NY
315-479-6023

North Country Mug
Cape Vincent, NY
315-773-1721

Suffolk Macintosh User Group
Stony Brook, NY
516-473-7175

D

North Carolina

Charlotte Apple Computer Club
Charlotte, NC
704-335-8661

Rural User Group
Brasstown, NC
704-837-7432

Ohio

Appleciders Of Cincinnati
Cincinnati, OH
513-741-4329

Buckeye Macintosh Group
Hilliard, OH
614-462-7066

Columbus Apple Core
Columbus, OH
614-268-1056

Future World Bbs
Akron, OH
216-773-9870

Gahanna Apple Users
Gahanna, OH
614-855-0937

Macincinnati
Cincinnati, OH
513-681-1647

Nautilus (A Division Of Metatec Corp)
Dublin, OH
614-761-2000

Oklahoma

Tulsa Users Of Macintosh Society
Tulsa, OK
918-621-2216

Oregon

Rogue Apple Ii Users Group
Ashland, OR
503-482-3377

Pennsylvania

Delaware Valley Apple Branch
Berwyn, PA
215-644-2690

Erie Apple Crunchers Inc.
Erie, PA
814-459-0992

Keystone Apple Core
East Berlin, PA
717-259-0827

Level Green Macintosh User Group
Trafford, PA
412-372-9258

Pennsylvania Apples
Boalsburg, PA
814-466-3322

Waynesboro Apple Core
Waynesboro, PA
717-762-1680

Rhode Island

Rhode Island Mug
Providence, RI
401-253-8528

Tennessee

Appleachian User's Group
Knoxville, TN
615-588-5406

D

Chattanooga Macintosh Users Group
Chattanooga, TN
615-755-4268

Texas

Apple Corps Of Dallas
Dallas, TX
214-238-1224

Central Texas Macintosh Users' Group
Waco, TX
817-755-3190

Clear Lake Area Machine Support
League City, TX
713-332-2398

Concho Valley Computer Support Group
San Angelo, TX
915-944-1688

Lone Star Mac-Online
Ft. Worth, TX
817-346-0885

Mac Office Girls Mug
San Antonio, TX
210-494-1004

Nasa Area Macintosh Users
Webster, TX
713-488-2262

Utah

Alpine Computing Microage Exec. Mug
Orem, UT
801-226-1510

Virginia

Greater Reston Area Macintosh Assoc.
Reston, VA
703-620-2686

Peninsula Apple Core
Williamsburg, VA
804-229-9339

Washington

Macintosh Downtown Business Ug
Lynnwood, WA
206-624-9329

Macintosh User Group Connection
Wenatchee, WA
509-663-1950

The Apple Franklin Laser Ug Of Spokane
Spokane, WA
509-624-1510

Wisconsin

Command-Option's
Lancaster, WI
608-723-6467

Double Click Mug
Milwaukee, WI
414-964-3147

Wisconsin Apple User Club
Wauwatosa, WI
414-771-6086

D

Index

U

V

About the Software That Accompanies This Book

We've chosen twenty programs reviewed in this book and included them on a disk. Here's a quick guide to help you install the contents of the disk onto your computer:

To Install the Programs

Insert the floppy disk into your Macintosh. Double-click the file "PROGRAMMER'S COOKBOOK INSTALLER." After the splash screen, you will see some text explaining what to do.Click the Continue button. Next, choose a location on your hard drive to which you can save the files. The entire set of files, when decompressed, takes up about 3 MB of disk space. After you click Okay, the files will be installed.

To Use the Software

Instructions for using the software are contained in the readme files that come with each program.To get a complete list of the software contained on the disk and for more information on the installation of the disk, turn to Appendix B"Try 'em Out for Size: Exploring the Disk."

Note: *Tech support for these programs is provided soley by the program's author. Contact names and registraion information can be found in Appendix B of this book. Please do not contact either Osborne/McGraw-Hill or the author of this book for tech support for any program contained on the disk. Register the programs with the program's authors, and they'll support you. If the disk is unreadable or fails to boot properly, call Osborne/McGraw-Hill at 510-549-6600. Any other problem with the disk must be addressed to the program's author.*

WARNING: BEFORE OPENING THE DISK PACKAGE, CAREFULLY READ THE TERMS AND CONDITIONS OF THE FOLLOWING DISK WARRANTY.

Disk Warranty

This software is protected by both United States copyright law and international copyright treaty provision. You must treat this software just like a book, except that you may copy it into a computer to be used and you may make archival copies of the software for the sole purpose of backing up our software and protecting your investment from loss. By saying, "just like a book," Osborne/McGraw-Hill means, for example, that this software may be used by any number of people and may be freely moved from one computer location to another, so long as there is no possibility of its being used at one location or on one computer while it is being used at another. Just as a book cannot be read by two different people in two different places at the same time, neither can the software be used by two different people in two different places at the same time (unless, of course, Osborne's copyright is being violated).

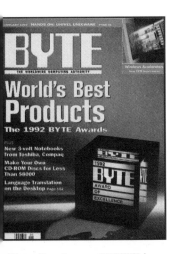